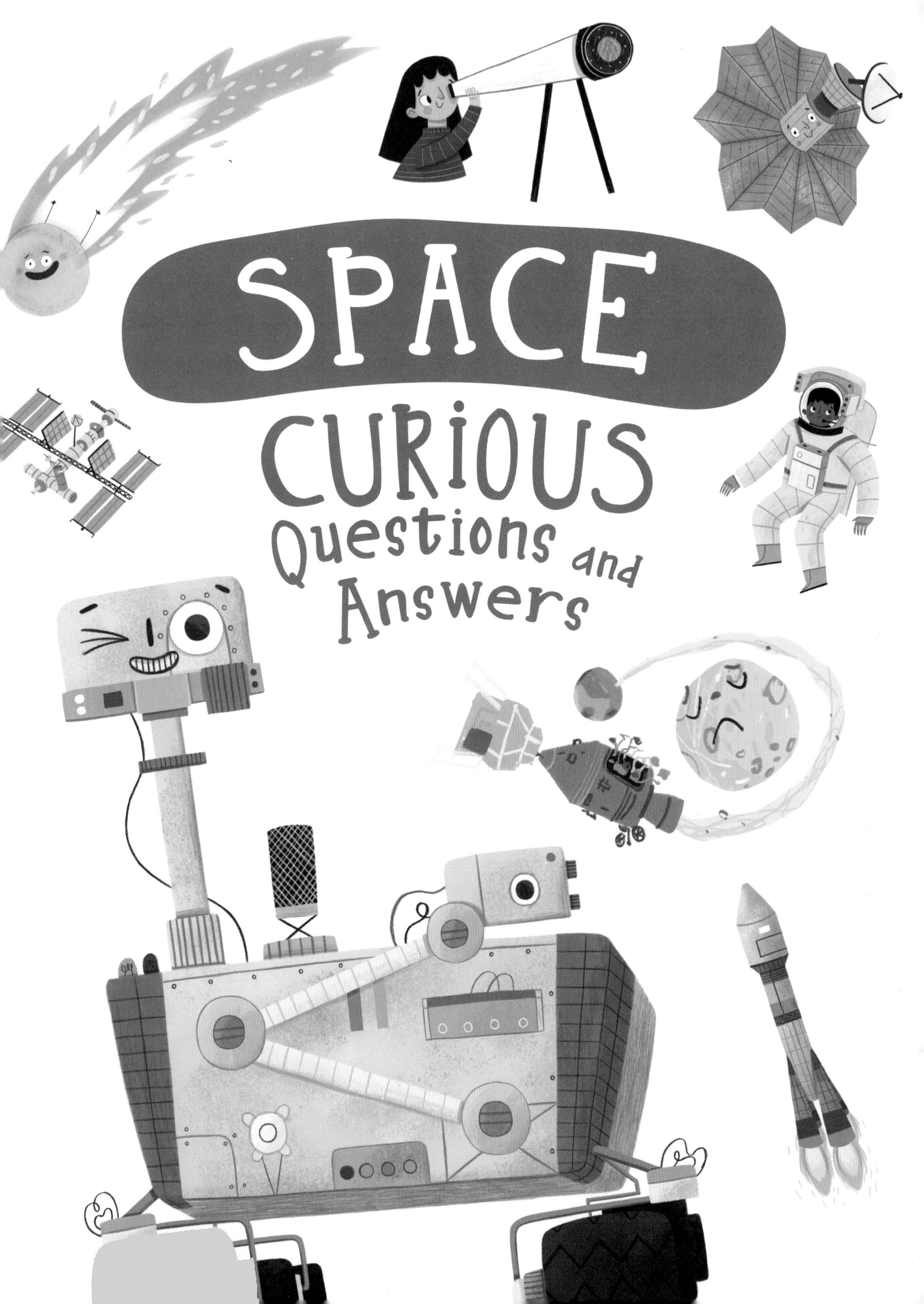

SPACE

CURIOUS Questions and Answers

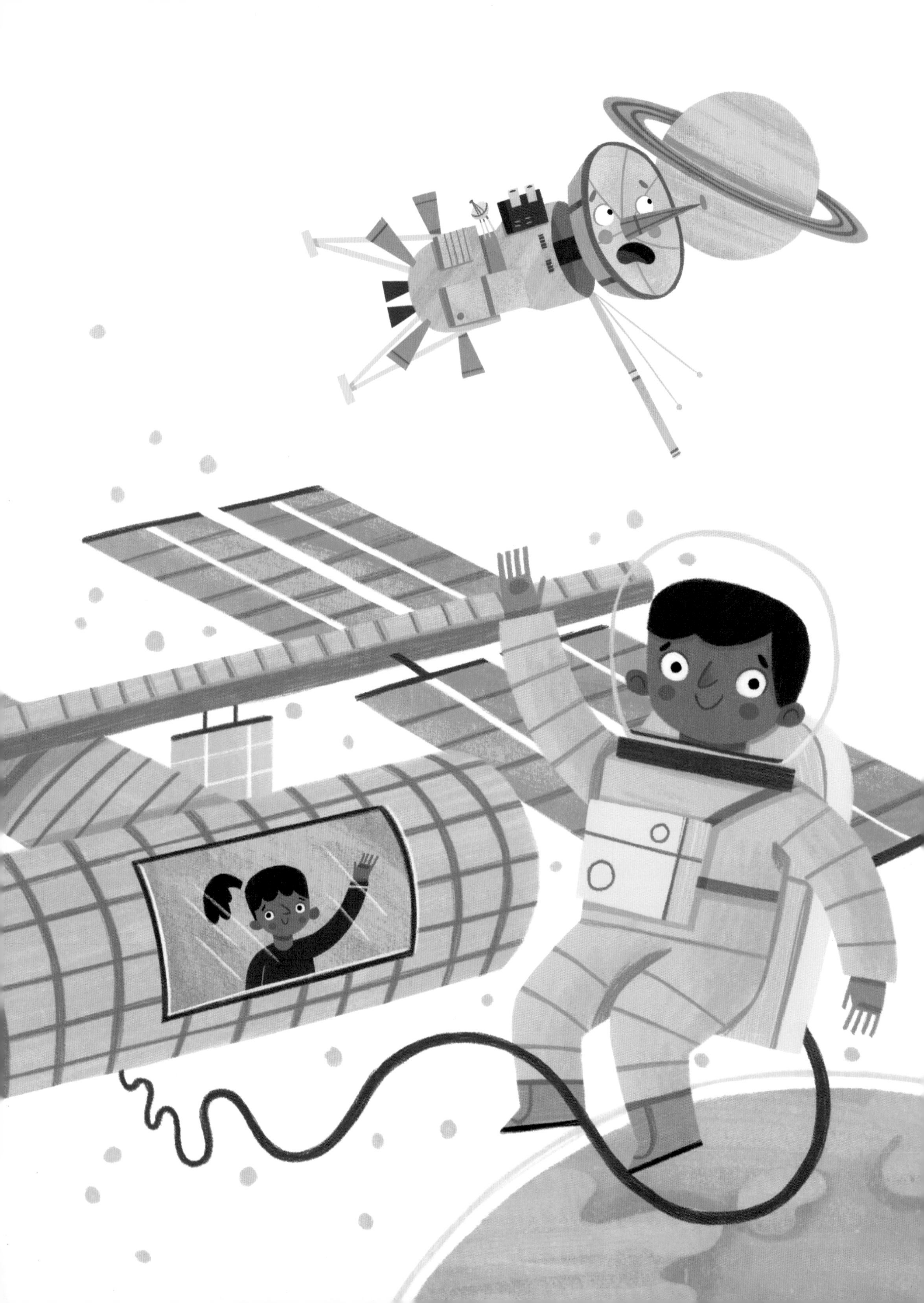

SPACE

CURIOUS Questions and Answers

Words by Sue Becklake, Ian Graham and Anne Rooney

Illustrations by Barbara Bakos, Ana Gomez, Lucy Semple and Pauline Reeves

Miles Kelly

First published in 2020 by Miles Kelly Publishing Ltd
Harding's Barn, Bardfield End Green, Thaxted, Essex, CM6 3PX, UK

4 6 8 10 9 7 5 3

Publishing Director Belinda Gallagher
Creative Director Jo Cowan
Editorial Director Rosie Neave
Editors Fran Bromage, Sarah Carpenter, Amy Johnson,
Design Managers Joe Jones, Simon Lee
Designers Craig Eaton, Andrea Slane
Image Manager Liberty Newton
Production Elizabeth Collins
Reprographics Stephan Davis
Assets Lorraine King

Cover Artist Leire Martín @ The Bright Agency

ISBN 978-1-78989-152-2

Printed in China

British Library Cataloguing-in-Publication Data
A catalogue record for this book is available from the British Library

Made with paper from a sustainable forest

www.mileskelly.net

CONTENTS

Do you prefer sunlight or moonlight?
What's the first thing you'd pack for a trip to outer space?
What's your favourite planet?

SOLAR SYSTEM

You're joining a space mission – what's your specialist skill?

Would you rather visit the Moon or Mars?

Where is the Solar System?

It's all around you. The Solar System is the Sun, eight planets and everything else that moves through space with the Sun.

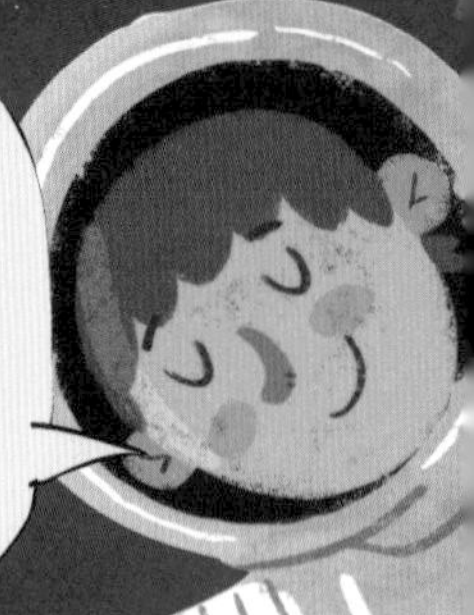

The planet we live on is called Earth. It's the third planet from the Sun.

Earth

Sun

In the middle of the Solar System is a star called the Sun.

Venus

Mercury

Planets

Planets are the giant things like the Earth that travel round the Sun. There are eight in our

The four planets closest to the Sun are small worlds made mostly of rock.

Moons

A moon is a small world that circles a bigger object – usually a planet. Earth has one, and it is made of rock

Asteroids

Asteroids are rocky worlds smaller than planets. There are millions of them.

Dwarf planets

Similar to planets in many ways, dwarf planets go round the Sun, but are not as big as planets.

How do you make a solar system?

Our Solar System began as a huge cloud of gas and dust in space.

①

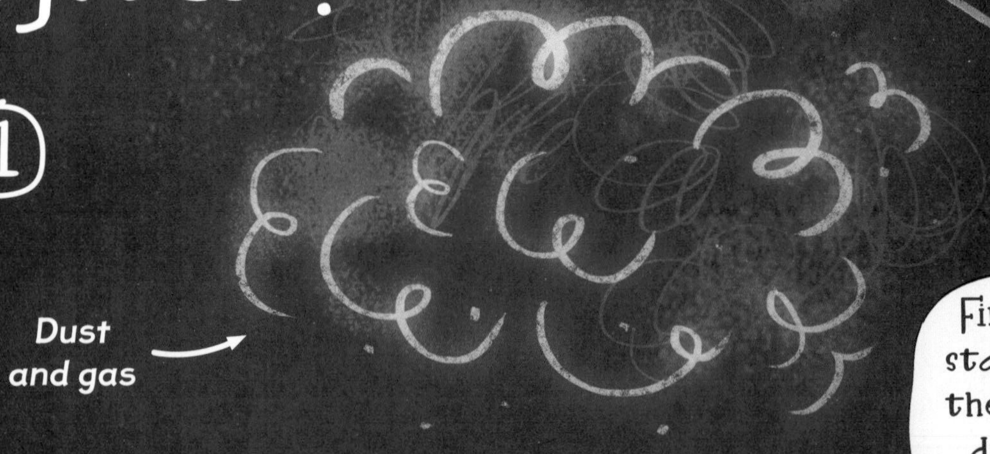

Dust and gas

How did the Solar System begin, and where did it come from?

First, an exploding star pushed against the cloud. The whole dusty cloud began to shrink.

③

So, there was a swirling disc of dust and gas – then what happened?

The dust and gas began to stick together, forming lumps that smashed into each other.

Lumps

2
Whoosh!
Flat disc
Why is the Solar System flat, like a plate?
As the cloud got smaller, it started to spin. Spinning flattened it out into a wide, thin disc.
4
How did the lumpy disc become the Sun and planets?
Huge energy built up in the centre of the disc, causing the lump in the middle to become the Sun. The biggest other lumps formed the planets.
Planets
Sun

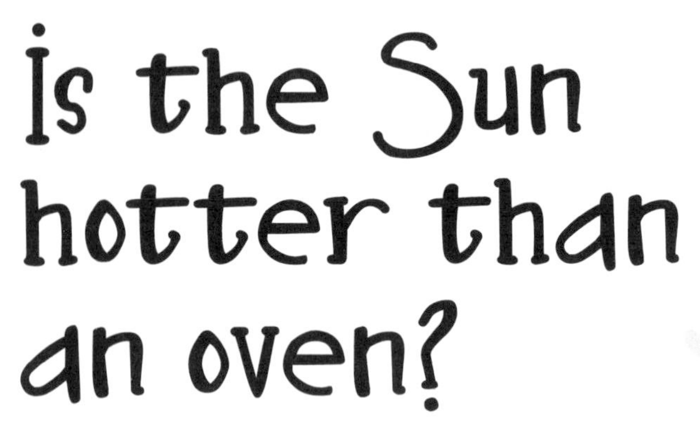

Is the Sun hotter than an oven?

The Sun's surface is over 20 times hotter than a regular oven! The centre is even hotter – thousands of times hotter than an oven. It would melt the oven!

NEVER NEVER look at the Sun. It's so bright and hot that it will hurt your eyes.

What is the Sun made of?

It's mostly made of stuff called hydrogen and helium. On Earth, hydrogen and helium are gases.

Why is the Sun bigger than other stars?

It isn't – the Sun is actually a small star. It looks much bigger than the other stars you see at night, because it is much closer to Earth than those other stars. They're all suns, but they are very far away.

Side-by-side with another star, I'm actually pretty tiny!

Scientists have found some suns that are 100 times bigger than the one in the Solar System!

Will the Sun be there forever?

No, but don't worry – it isn't going to disappear any time soon. The Sun should be there for another 5000 million years.

Where does the Sun go at night?

The Sun doesn't go anywhere – it's the Earth that is moving!

Our planet spins around an invisible line called the axis. It's daytime for you when the side you live on faces the Sun.

This spinning motion makes it look to us on Earth as if the Sun rises in the morning, crosses the sky, and then disappears at sunset.

Axis

N

Light rays

S

Sunset

ZZZ

Why is a day 24 hours long?

It takes 24 hours for Earth to spin around once, and we call this a day.

Why do we have seasons?

Because Earth's axis is tilted. This means different bits of Earth get the Sun's direct rays at different times during Earth's orbit (journey around the Sun).

What is the Equator?

It's an invisible line that circles Earth. It divides it into a northern (top) half and southern (bottom) half.

Equator

N

S

In June, it's summer in the north and winter in the south.

In March, it's spring in the north, and autumn in the south.

In December, it's winter in the north and summer in the south.

In September, it's autumn in the north and spring in the south.

What is a year?

A year is the time it takes for the Earth to complete one orbit of the Sun.

Did you know?

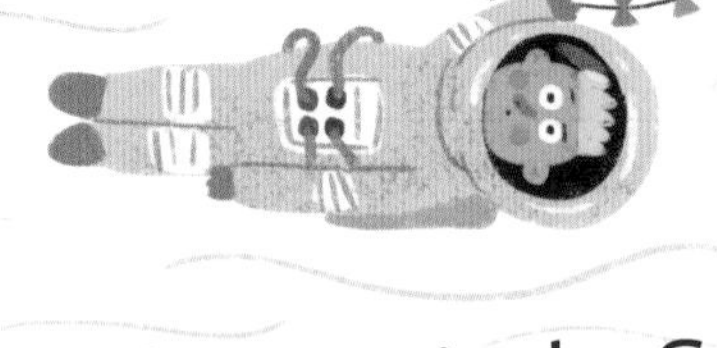

Jupiter has a huge storm called the Great Red Spot – it's about three times bigger than **Earth**.

Neptune is the Solar System's windiest planet, with winds ten times faster than the worst hurricanes on **Earth**.

Saturn is famous for its rings, but **Jupiter**, **Uranus** and **Neptune** have them too.

My rings are easy to see, because they're made of pieces of ice. Sunlight bounces off the ice and lights them up.

Our rings are thin, dark and dusty so they're hard to see.

The centre of the **Earth** is made of metal so hot that some of it has melted and turned to liquid.

You can jump six times higher on the **Moon** than you can on **Earth**.

Jupiter's moon **Ganymede** is the biggest moon in the Solar System – even bigger than the planet **Mercury**.

Dust storms are common on **Mars**. The sky there is pinky red, as so much red dust is blown about by the wind.

If you know where to look, you can see five planets without a telescope – **Mercury**, **Venus**, **Mars**, **Jupiter** and **Saturn**.

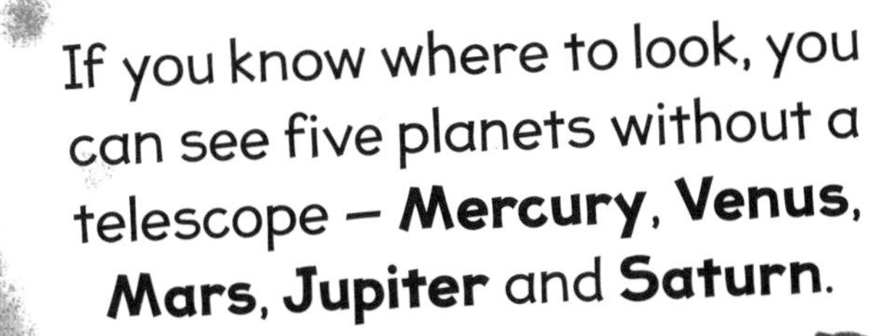

They are so far away they look like stars.

I'm only about half the width of the USA!

Astronauts who visited the **Moon** brought 382 kilograms of Moon rocks back with them.

Pluto was the Solar System's ninth planet – until 2006 when scientists decided to call it a dwarf planet instead.

There are between two and five solar eclipses every year.

Giant **Jupiter** spins so fast it has the shortest day of any planet – just 9 hours 55 minutes.

A solar eclipse happens when the **Moon** passes in front of the **Sun**. The Moon's shadow then moves across **Earth**, causing darkness to fall.

Are other planets like Earth?

Earth and the other three planets closest to the Sun are alike in some ways, but no other planet is exactly like Earth.

Why is it always so hot here?

Mercury is very hot because it's the closest planet to the Sun. It's smaller than Earth and it looks like the Moon.

Mercury

Why am I known as Earth's twin planet?

Venus

Venus and Earth are similar in size and structure – but the two planets look very different. Venus is wrapped in thick clouds of acid. They trap heat, so Venus is even hotter than Mercury.

Earth
Why am I blue?
Mars
Why am I called the Red Planet?

Water covers 70 percent of Earth's surface. Sunlight contains all the colours of the rainbow. When sunlight shines on Earth, the water reflects the blue part of the light back into space.

Mars is a small world about half the size of Earth. It looks red all over because its soil and rocks are full of rusty iron. Mars is a rusty planet.

What are the outer planets like?

The four planets farthest from the Sun – Jupiter, Saturn, Uranus and Neptune – couldn't be more different from Earth. They are giant worlds made of gas and liquid.

Where did my rings come from?
Jupiter
How big am I?
Saturn

Jupiter is the biggest planet in the Solar System. It's so big that more than a thousand Earths would fit inside it!

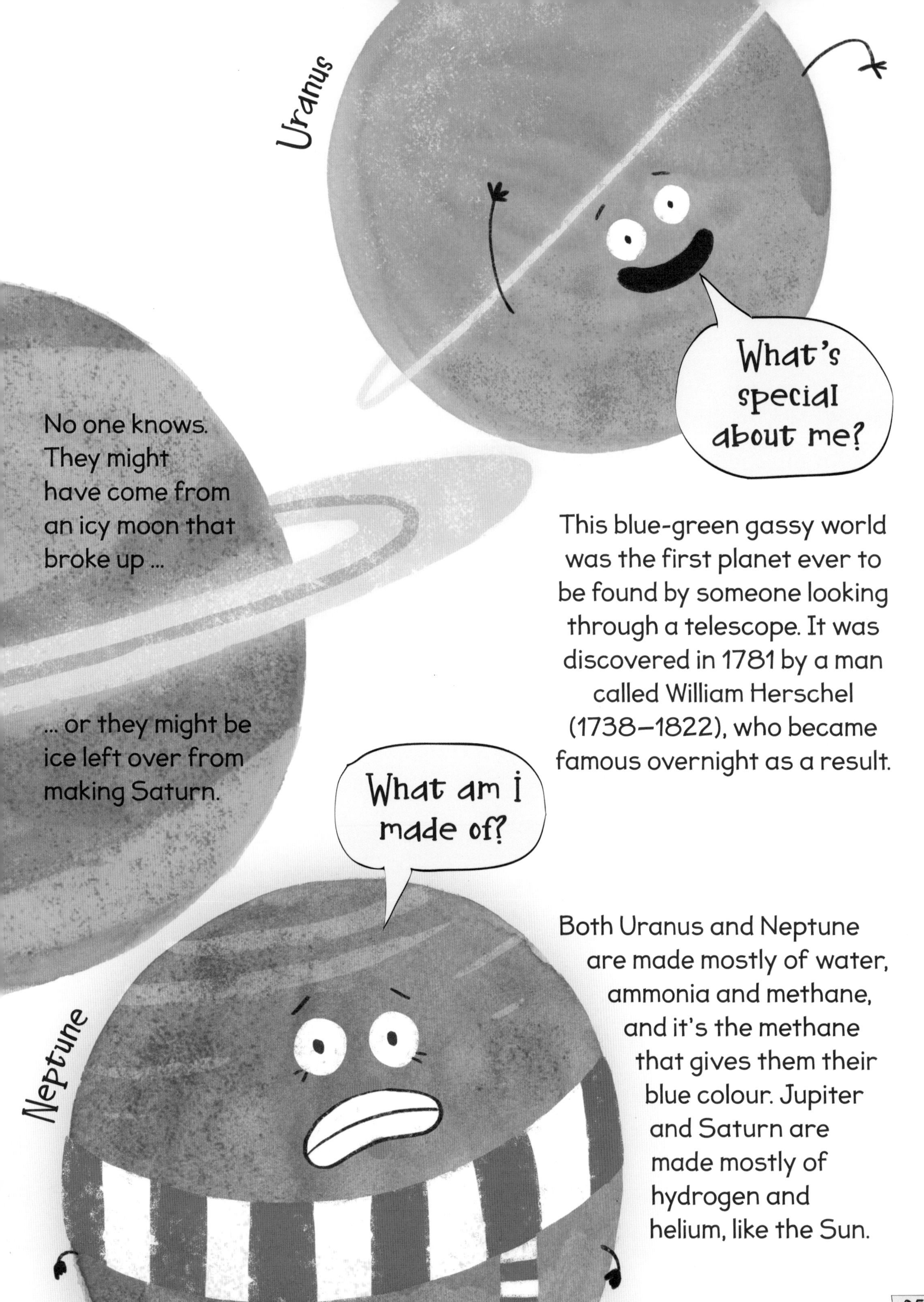

Uranus
What's special about me?
No one knows. They might have come from an icy moon that broke up ...
... or they might be ice left over from making Saturn.
What am I made of?
Neptune

This blue-green gassy world was the first planet ever to be found by someone looking through a telescope. It was discovered in 1781 by a man called William Herschel (1738–1822), who became famous overnight as a result.

Both Uranus and Neptune are made mostly of water, ammonia and methane, and it's the methane that gives them their blue colour. Jupiter and Saturn are made mostly of hydrogen and helium, like the Sun.

Do planets ever crash into each other?

Almost never. Billions of years ago, a planet the size of Mars crashed into Earth and sent lots of rock flying out into space. Can you guess what happened next?

1. A planet called Theia crashed into Earth.

2. The crash threw lots of rocks into space around Earth.

3. The rocks in space came together and became the Moon.

The Moon is the only place beyond Earth that humans have set foot on.

What's it like on the Moon?

The Moon is very dry and covered with grey dust. There are mountains, but there is no air, and the sky is always inky black.

Why is the Moon covered with craters?

These dents are made when rocks flying through space hit the Moon.

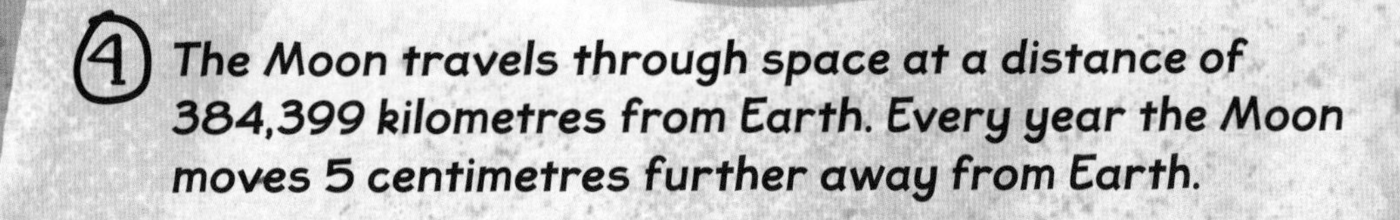

4 *The Moon travels through space at a distance of 384,399 kilometres from Earth. Every year the Moon moves 5 centimetres further away from Earth.*

Would you rather?

Would you rather discover a new planet, like **William Herschel** did...

...or work out that all the planets in the Solar System orbit the Sun, like **Nicolaus Copernicus** did?

Would you rather live on **Earth** for your whole life, or spend your whole life in a **space station** where you could float about weightless?

If I lived on Mercury I'd be sixteen!
If I lived on Neptune I'd be younger than you!

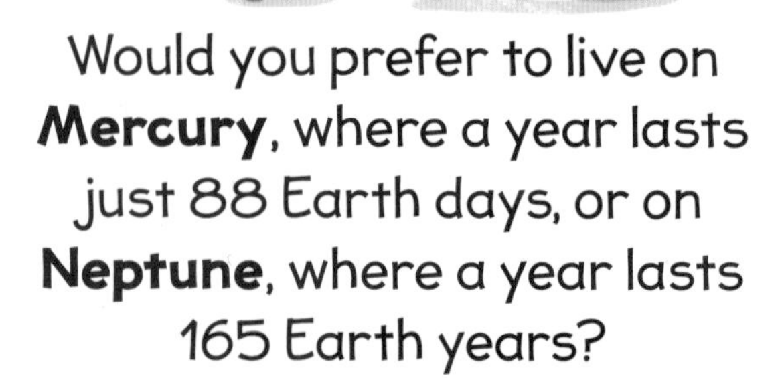

Would you prefer to live on **Mercury**, where a year lasts just 88 Earth days, or on **Neptune**, where a year lasts 165 Earth years?

Would you rather kick a ball really far on the **Moon** or make a red sandcastle on **Mars**?

Which part of astronaut training would you rather do:

Work in a huge tank of water to practise **space walks**...

...or take a spin to get a feel for **extreme forces**?

If you had to name a new planet, would you rather call it **Aether**, after the Greek god of light, or **Erebus**, the god of darkness?

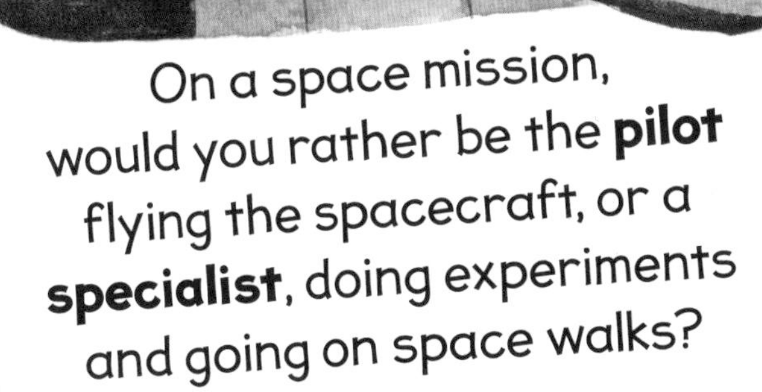

On a space mission, would you rather be the **pilot** flying the spacecraft, or a **specialist**, doing experiments and going on space walks?

Would you rather live on Uranus in **winter**, when the Sun doesn't rise for 20 years, or in **summer**, when it doesn't set for 20 years?

Would you rather slow down **Earth's** spin so days are longer, or move Earth closer to the **Sun** so that the weather is warmer?

What are shooting stars?

They're not stars! They're small pieces of rock that fly through space and into the air around Earth. Rubbing against the air heats them until they glow. They are also called meteors.

When lots of meteors appear in the sky, it's called a meteor shower.

Where do shooting stars go?

The smallest burn up and disappear. Others sometimes fall all the way down to the ground. If they land on Earth, they're called meteorites.

What happens when a big meteorite hits Earth?

It makes a hole in the ground called a crater. A famous crater in Arizona, USA, was made by a meteorite 50 metres across that hit the ground 50,000 years ago.

Why do comets have long, bright tails?
Comets are like giant dusty snowballs in space. If they fly near the Sun, some of the ice turns to gas and bursts out, carrying dust with it. The dust forms a tail that is lit up by sunlight.

How big are space rocks?

The biggest rocks in space are asteroids. Some can be up to 1000 kilometres across. Most asteroids are found in the Asteroid Belt between Mars and Jupiter.

How many?

–200° Celsius:

The average temperature on the Solar System's coldest planet, Neptune.

178 moons have been found going around planets so far. More might be found in future.

Life appeared on Earth about **4,000,000,000** years ago.

7,500,000,000 The number of people living on Earth.

0 The number of moons that the planets Mercury and Venus have.

The Solar System is about **4,600,000,000** years old.

The Solar System's tallest mountain is Olympus Mons on Mars. It's nearly **3** times the height of the tallest mountain on Earth, Mount Everest.

How many astronauts have walked on the Moon?

12

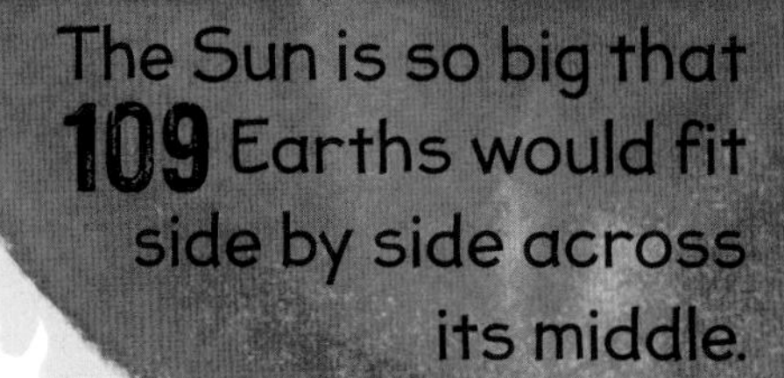

The Sun is so big that **109** Earths would fit side by side across its middle.

150 million kilometres: the distance from Earth to the Sun.

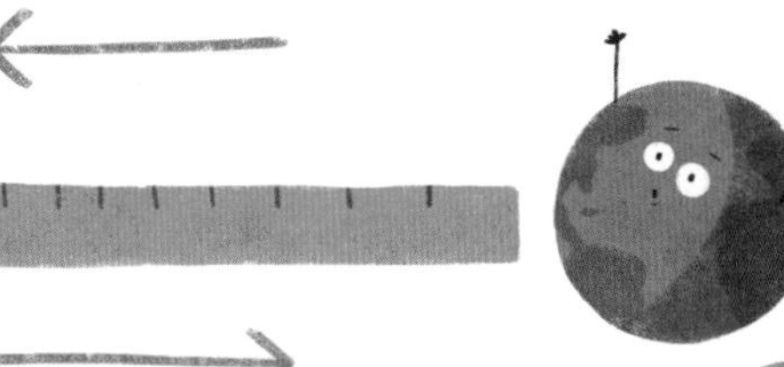

Halley's Comet appears in the sky every **76** years.

Just over **8** minutes: the amount of time it takes for sunlight to reach Earth.

165

The number of Earth years it takes the farthest planet, Neptune, to go once around the Sun.

3

...the number of days it takes astronauts to fly to the Moon in a spacecraft.

There are **5** dwarf planets in the Solar System. They are called...

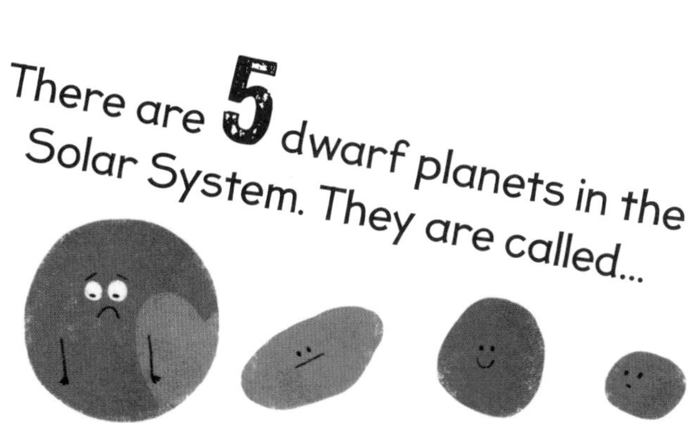

Eris *Pluto* *Haumea* *Makemake* *Ceres*

How do we know about other planets?

No human has ever visited another planet, but we learn about them by sending robot spacecraft to study them. We have sent more spacecraft to Mars than any other planet.

I used my robotic arm to scoop up Martian soil to find out what it's made of.
Solar panels provide power
Robotic arm
Phoenix lander

Do spacecraft land on other planets?

Yes! Spacecraft that land on a planet are called landers. They take photographs of the surface and measure things like the temperature and wind speed. A spacecraft called Phoenix landed on Mars in 2008.

How do we get good photos of Mars?

Mars Reconnaissance Orbiter
Robot spacecraft like me are called orbiters. We fly round and round it, like tiny moons. As we circle, we take photos and send them back to Earth by radio.

What is a rover?

Some of the spacecraft on Mars have wheels so that they can move around and explore more of the planet. They're called rovers. A rover called Curiosity landed on Mars in 2012.

Special instruments measure temperatures, wind speeds, radiation, and much more

My mission is to investigate Martian climate and geology, to find out whether Mars can support any life.
Curiosity

Is there life anywhere else?

Erm... hello? Is anyone at home?

Not that we know of – the search goes on. The spacecraft we have sent to other planets have been searching for signs of life there.

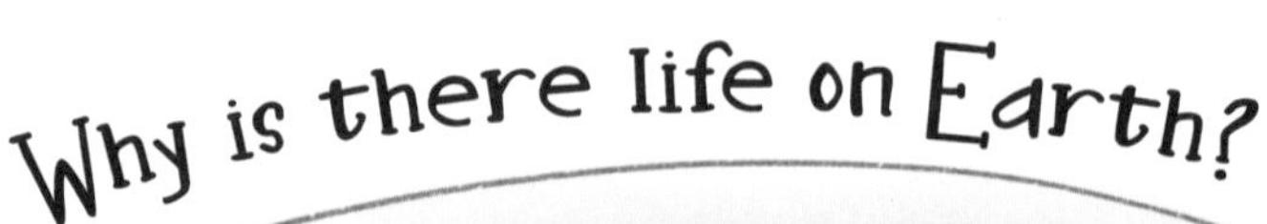
Why is there life on Earth?

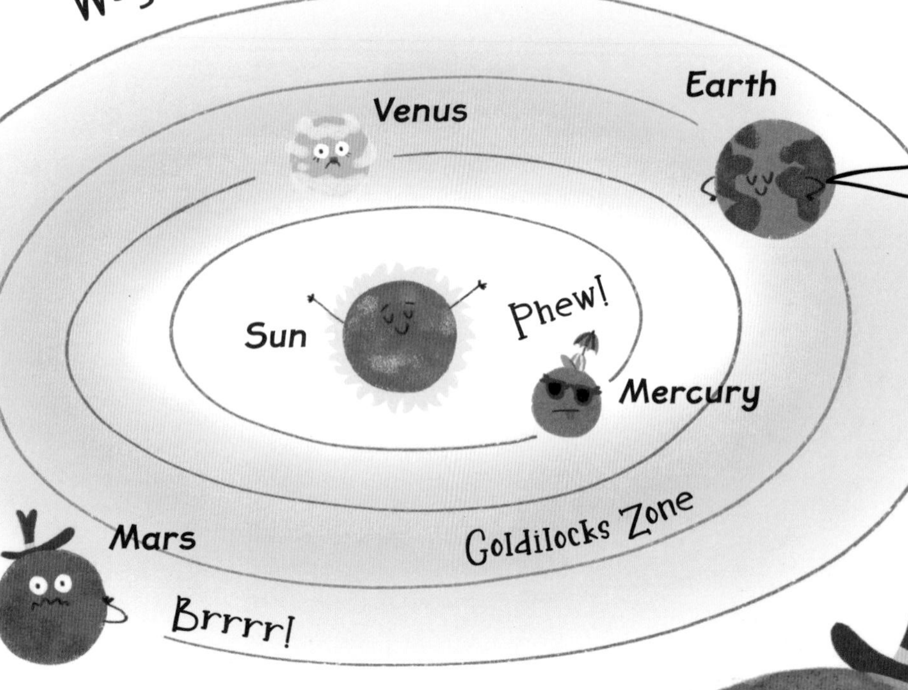
Venus
Earth
Sun
Phew!
Mercury
Mars
Goldilocks Zone
Brrrr!

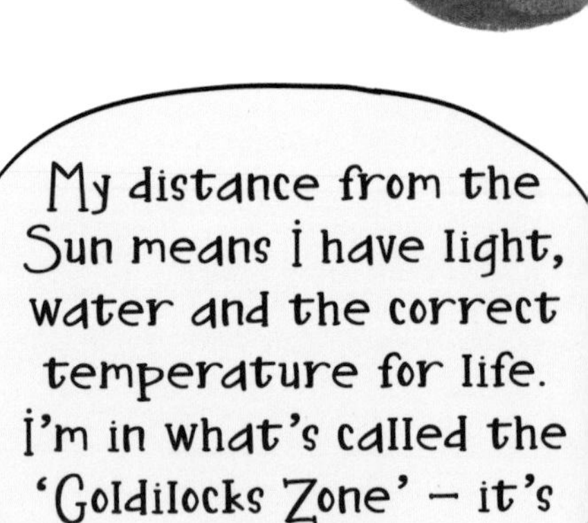
My distance from the Sun means I have light, water and the correct temperature for life. I'm in what's called the 'Goldilocks Zone' – it's just right.

Why did people think aliens lived on Mars?

When people first used telescopes to study Mars they thought they saw lines on its surface. The idea spread that these were canals, made by aliens.

When spacecraft visited Mars, they found a dry, dusty planet with no canal – or aliens.

Is there water anywhere else in the Solar System?

Scientists think there may be oceans beneath the surfaces of some of Jupiter and Saturn's icy moons. Future missions will search for life there.

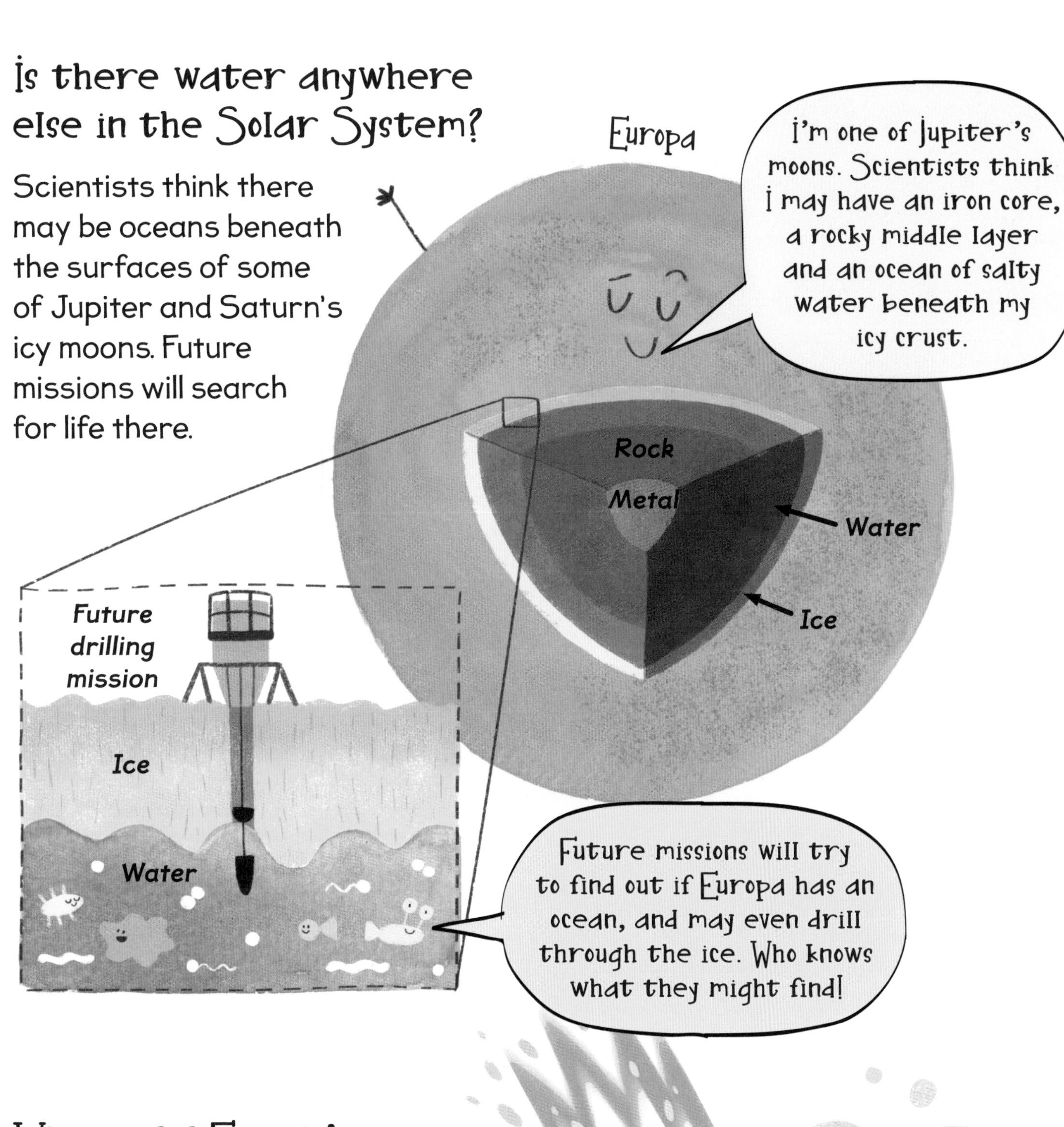

Europa
I'm one of Jupiter's moons. Scientists think I may have an iron core, a rocky middle layer and an ocean of salty water beneath my icy crust.
Rock
Metal
Water
Ice
Future drilling mission
Ice
Water
Future missions will try to find out if Europa has an ocean, and may even drill through the ice. Who knows what they might find!

Where did Earth's water come from?

Some of it was already in the rocks that formed the Earth. The rest arrived as ice on comets and other space rocks that crashed into Earth soon after it formed.

A compendium of questions

Why is Earth called Earth?

It comes from an ancient word meaning land. Earth is the only planet that wasn't named after an ancient Greek or Roman god.

Which moon is the weirdest?

Hmmm... maybe Saturn's moon Enceladus. It spews jets of gas and ice from its south pole!

The jets come from an ocean of water beneath Enceladus' icy surface

Are there rainbows on the Moon?

Sunlight and rain are both needed for a rainbow. There is no rain on the Moon, so you will never see a rainbow there.

Why is the Earth's sky blue?

As sunlight travels through air, the blue part of the light is scattered in all directions, so the sky looks blue.

Where is the best view of the Sun?

Standing on Mercury when it is at its closest to the Sun, the Sun would appear more than three times as large as it does from Earth.

I'm only 58 million kilometres away!

Why aren't planets square?

Planets are round because of gravity. This special force pulls everything inwards, forming a ball shape.

Is there lightning on other planets?

Yes. Spacecraft have seen lightning storms on Venus, Jupiter and Saturn.

Can a spacecraft land on a gas planet?

No – and they can't fly through them either! The extreme temperature and pressure inside would crush a spacecraft.

Scientists think Jupiter's core could be up to 50,000° Celsius! Phew!

Why are the planets different colours?

Because planets are made of different mixtures of rocks and gases that reflect light in different ways.

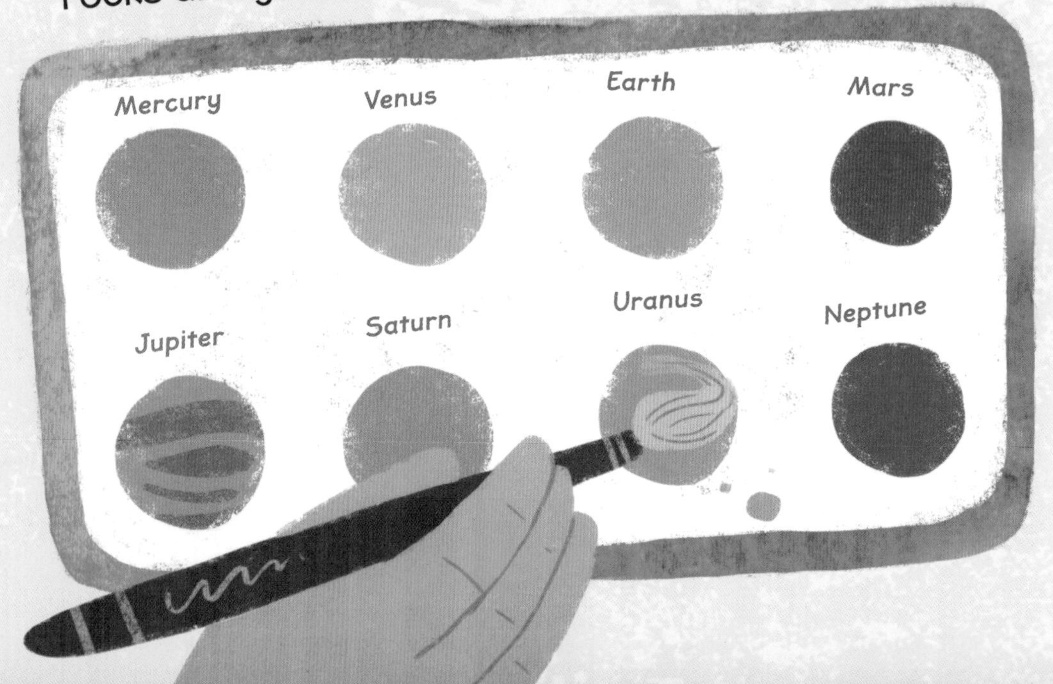

Who is the Man in the Moon?

Some people think marks on the surface look like a face. Others think they can see the shape of a rabbit.

When did the first spacecraft go to the Moon?

In 1959, Luna 2 became the first spacecraft to crash-land there – no astronauts were onboard.

Are all the stars part of our Solar System?

No – the Sun is our only star. All the others are outside our Solar System.

Many other stars have their own families of planets.

Why do the planets spin?

The giant cloud of dust and gas that formed the Solar System started spinning as it shrank. The planets that formed from it carried on spinning.

Would you rather be an astronomer or an astronaut?
What noise do you think a rocket launch makes?
Who's your best friend?

Can you see the Moon right now?
If you were a spacecraft, where would you go?

THE MOON

What would you say if you met an alien on the Moon?

What is a moon?

A moon is a rocky body that orbits (moves around) a bigger object. Most planets in our Solar System have moons. Earth has one, which we simply call 'the Moon'.

I'm an artificial satellite, put into space by humans.
Moon's orbit

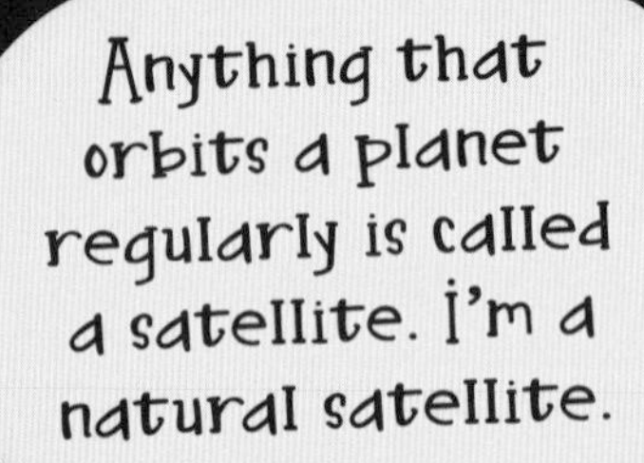

Anything that orbits a planet regularly is called a satellite. I'm a natural satellite.

The Moon
Axis
Direction of the Moon's spin

How big is our Moon?

The Moon is small enough that it would fit inside Earth fifty times over. It's still the fifth biggest moon in the Solar System, though!

Does the Moon move?

It orbits Earth, and it moves with Earth around the Sun. The Moon also spins, turning on its axis (an imaginary line through the centre). It takes the same amount of time to turn once on its axis as to orbit Earth once (about 28 days).

The Moon is kept in orbit by gravity, a force that draws objects with mass towards each other. The pull of my gravity keeps the Moon from escaping into space.
Earth
Axis
Direction of Earth's spin
= 10,000 kilometres
Earth

Is it far away?

Pretty far! The Moon is about 384,400 kilometres away from Earth. But it doesn't travel in a perfect circle, so sometimes it's a bit further away and sometimes a bit closer.

Where did the Moon come from?

It formed 4.5 billion years ago, when Earth was very new.

① A planet about the size of Mars, which has been named Theia, smashed into Earth.

② The energy of the crash melted a large amount of rocky Earth and Theia, and mixed them together.

(3) Some of the molten (liquid) rock fell back to Earth and became part of our planet, but some was thrown out into space. It cooled, turning back into hard rock.

(4) The bits of rock whizzed around Earth, bumping into each other. Eventually, all the lumps pulled together and fused...

What's inside the Moon?

Mostly rock. In the centre, there is a small core made of metal, mostly iron. It's surrounded by a layer of hot, semi-molten metal.

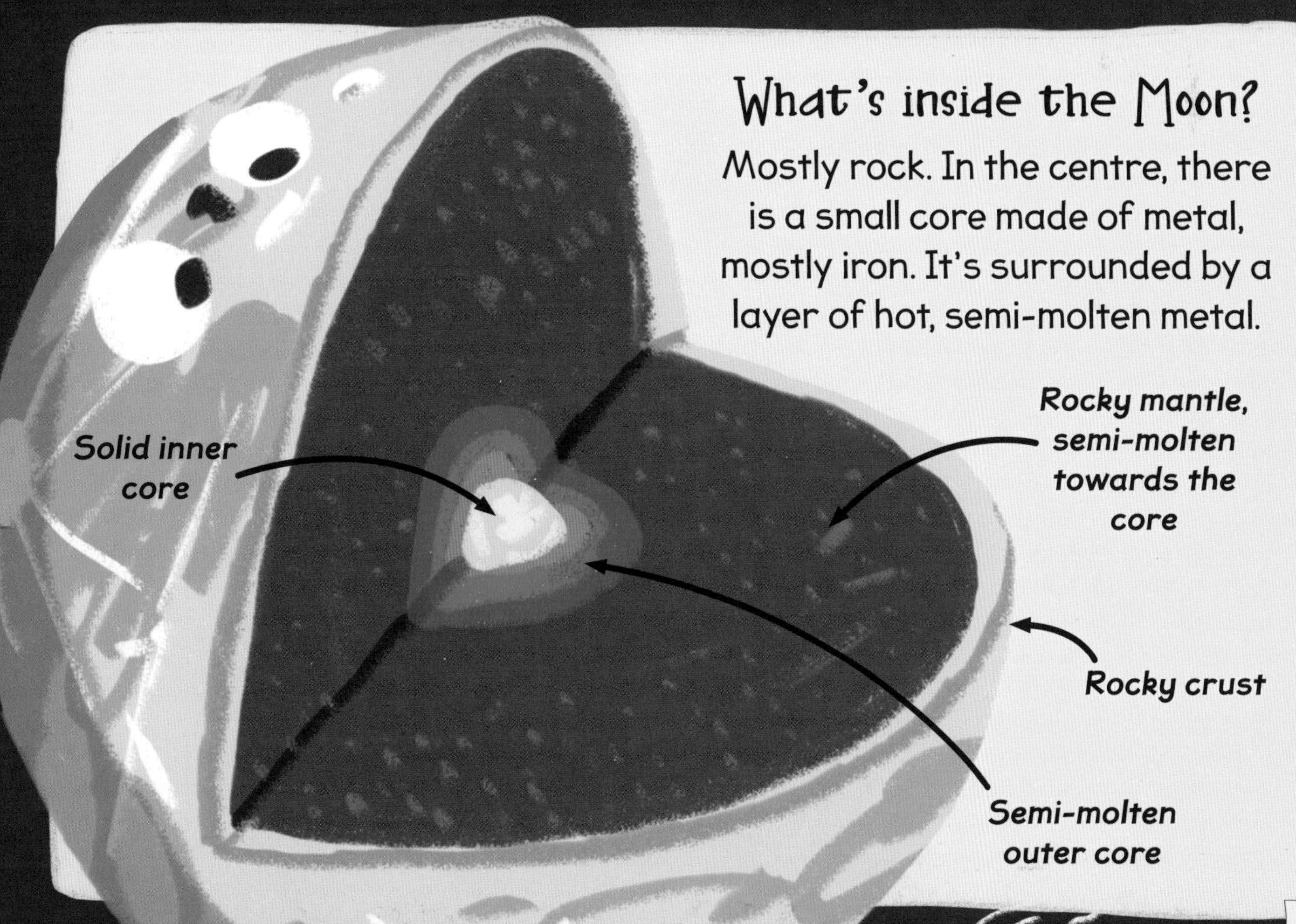

Are there mountains on the Moon?

Yes! The Moon's landscape is made up of mountains, craters and flat plains. The surface is rocky, covered with a deep layer of dust called regolith.

Is it hot or cold?

Both! It's scorching in the daytime when the Moon faces the Sun – it can be 127° Celsius. But it gets down to -173° Celsius at night. Daytime and night-time each last about two weeks, so any spot has lots of time to get hot or cold.

How can you jump so high?
Gravity is much weaker on the Moon, so people can jump easily and don't fall as quickly. A human can jump about 3 metres high and stay up for around 4 seconds.

Can you see the Sun and stars?

You can see the Sun in the daytime and the stars at night, just as you can on Earth. In daytime, the Sun is too bright for the stars to be visible. At night, the stars are dim as light reflected from Earth makes them hard to see.

You can also see Earth from the Moon, as long as you stand on the side facing Earth! It doesn't move across the Moon's sky, it hangs in one place all the time.

How many?

On the Moon, there are **500 million** craters that are more than 10 metres across.

Regolith on the Moon's surface is **2–8** metres deep.

It took Apollo 11 **51** hours **49** minutes to reach the Moon.

214

The number of known planetary moons in the Solar System.

12

The number of astronauts who have stood on the Moon.

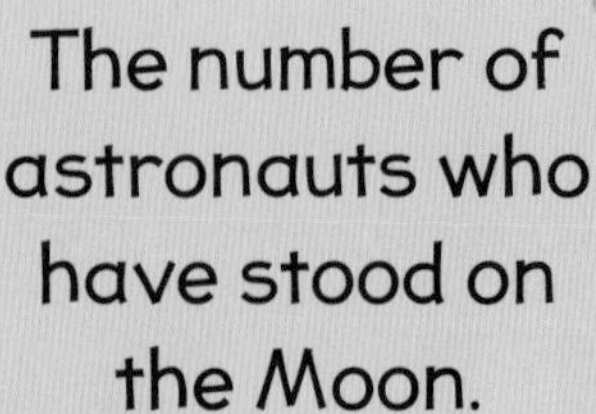

1737 The diameter (distance across) of the Moon in kilometres.

Neil Armstrong spent a total of **2** hours **12** minutes on the Moon's surface (outside the lander).

Eugene Cernan of Apollo 17 spent the longest time outside the lander, a total of **22** hours **5** minutes.

The Apollo 17 Moon buggy was driven the furthest, over **35** kilometres.

$25.8 billion The cost of the whole Apollo program ($194.3 billion at today's prices).

The Moon's gravity is **1/6** of Earth's gravity.

5268

The diameter in kilometres of the largest moon in the Solar System, Jupiter's moon Ganymede – it's bigger than the planet Mercury!

Ganymede

The Apollo missions brought back **382** kilograms of Moon rock.

Why do we only see one side of the Moon?

The Moon takes as long to turn once on its axis as it takes to orbit Earth. This means the same side of the Moon is always facing us – this is called tidal locking.

What is the far side like?

It's very different from the near side. The far side has many more small craters, and even craters within the craters. It has very few flat plains, and its colouring is more irregular.

Has anyone seen the far side?

It can only be seen in photos and from space. It was first seen by humans in 1968, when the Apollo 8 spacecraft went round the Moon. A Chinese spacecraft, Chang'e 4, landed on the far side in 2019 and took the first ground-based photos.

What is a crater?

A crater is a round dent with sloping sides. The Moon is covered in craters. They are caused by meteors crashing into the surface and gouging out holes.

We've been causing craters for billions of years, on the Moon as well as on planets and other moons.

1 *A meteor speeds towards the Moon.*

2 *The impact causes a shockwave, which blasts a hole in the surface.*

3 *Moon rock pushed out of the way is forced upwards. The meteor is destroyed.*

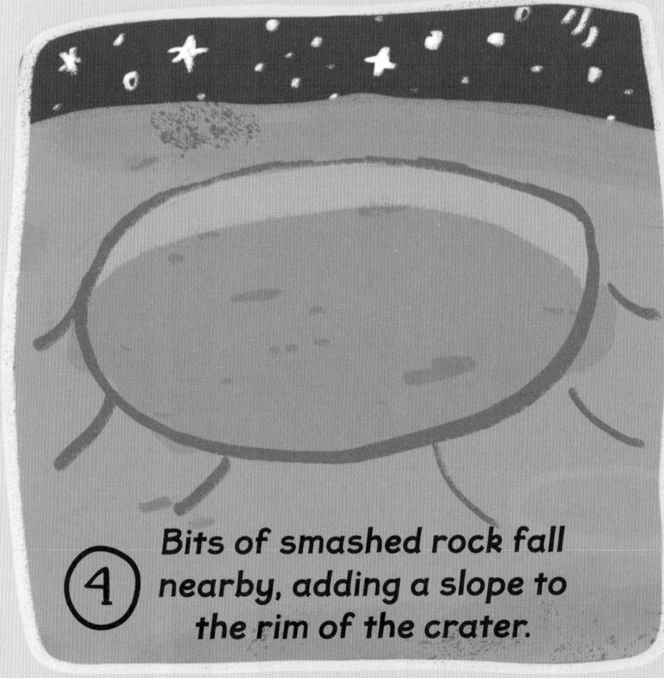

4 *Bits of smashed rock fall nearby, adding a slope to the rim of the crater.*

Do meteors hit both sides of the Moon?

Yes, but the near side has far fewer craters. The near side's surface is much thinner, so meteor impacts long ago broke through it. Hot, liquid rock (magma) from inside the Moon flooded out and hardened, smoothing the craters and forming the plains.

The surface on the far side is too thick to break, so its craters never healed.

Will the craters ever disappear?

The Moon doesn't have wind or flowing water, so there is nothing to get rid of the craters. Once the inside of the Moon cooled, craters could no longer be filled in by magma.

When meteors hit Earth, they usually burn up in the atmosphere. The Moon has no atmosphere, so meteors crash into the surface.

Did you know?

The Chang'e 4 spacecraft grew the first plant on the Moon – a **cotton plant** – inside a special container. It survived for 14 Earth days.

An explosion during the flight of **Apollo 13** damaged the spacecraft, so the crew had to loop around the Moon and return without landing.

Many spacecraft have orbited or landed on the Moon since I did!

There are **moonquakes** (like earthquakes). Some are caused by Earth's gravity pulling at the Moon's insides.

The first spacecraft to land on the Moon was the Soviet craft **Luna 2** on 13 September, 1959. It crashed into the surface (on purpose!).

Footprints on the Moon will stay there unless disturbed. They are just slowly worn away by meteoric dust hitting the Moon.

As far as we can tell, **nothing** has ever lived on the Moon.

The Moon is slowly moving further from Earth, at a rate of about **4 centimetres** a year.

Bye!

Apollo 15 astronaut David Scott dropped a **hammer** and a **feather** on the Moon to show they both fall at the same speed when there is no air.

We were left behind to save weight for the return journey.

The 12 **full moons** of the year have names: wolf, snow, worm, pink, flower, strawberry, buck, sturgeon, harvest, hunter's, beaver and cold moons.

Hoooooowl!

Astronauts left all their **personal waste** in bags on the Moon – and lots of other rubbish and bits of spacecraft.

The Moon's **plains** have names such as Sea of Cleverness, Serpent Sea and Sea of Waves.

Its **craters** include some named Billy, Carol, Mavis...

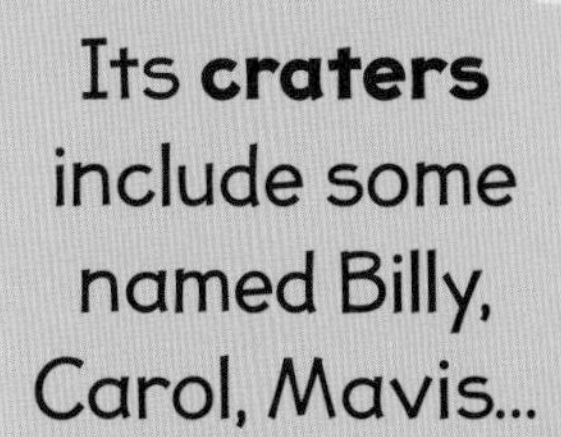

...and Bruce!

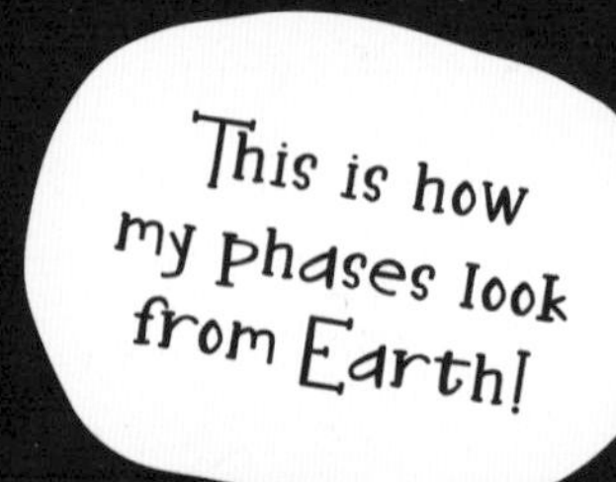

This is how my phases look from Earth!

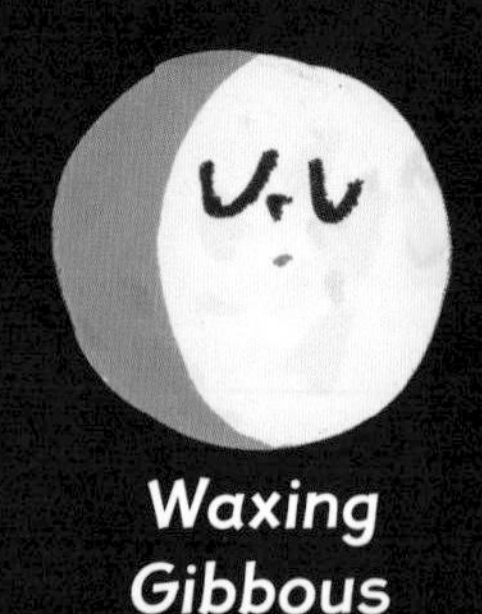

Does the Moon change shape?

It seems to change shape, but it doesn't really. As it moves around Earth, different parts are lit by the Sun. The changes are called phases.

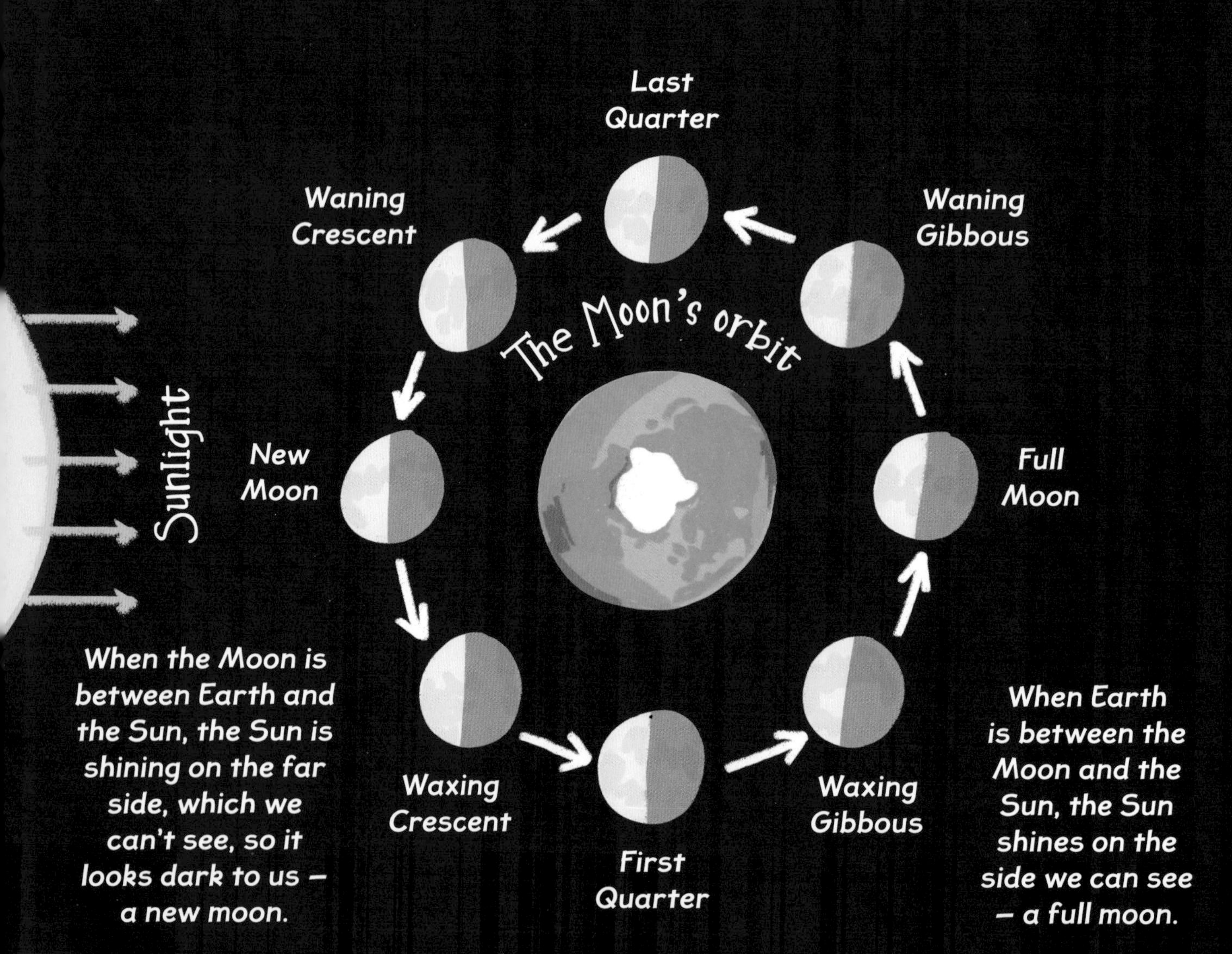

When the Moon is between Earth and the Sun, the Sun is shining on the far side, which we can't see, so it looks dark to us – a new moon.

When Earth is between the Moon and the Sun, the Sun shines on the side we can see – a full moon.

Full Moon

Waning Gibbous

Last Quarter

Waning Crescent

I seem to shine because I reflect the sunlight that falls on me. I don't make my own light, like the Sun or other stars.

Why is the Moon sometimes red?

During a total lunar eclipse, the Sun is directly behind Earth and so the Moon is in Earth's shadow. Some of the sunlight passing through Earth's atmosphere is bent towards the Moon, turning it red.

Can the Moon block out the Sun?

Yes – during a solar eclipse. When the Moon moves between Earth and the Sun and they line up exactly, the Moon's shadow moves over Earth. In some places, it blocks out the Sun completely for a few minutes – a total eclipse.

Total solar eclipse

During a total solar eclipse, parts of Earth are plunged into darkness.

How does the Moon move the sea?

The Moon's gravity pulls at Earth's oceans. This makes the water pile up on the side nearest the Moon, creating a bulge. The water also piles up to make a bulge on the other side.

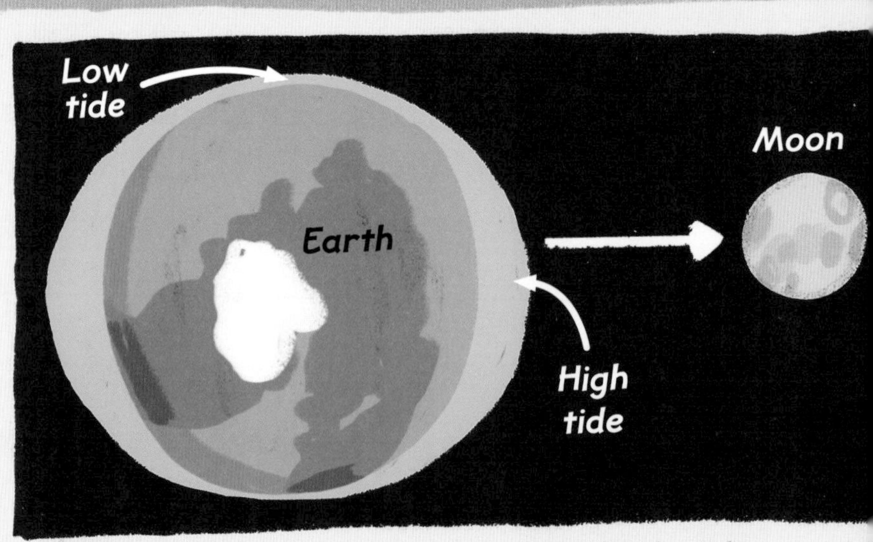

The bulge sweeps round Earth, pulled along by the Moon's gravity as it orbits, and also by Earth turning underneath. This creates the tides.

Most coasts have two high tides a day, one when nearest the Moon and one when furthest from it.

What causes very high and low tides?

The Sun also helps make the tides. When the Sun and Moon are lined up (at full moon and new moon), they pull in the same direction. This creates extra-high and low tides, called spring tides.

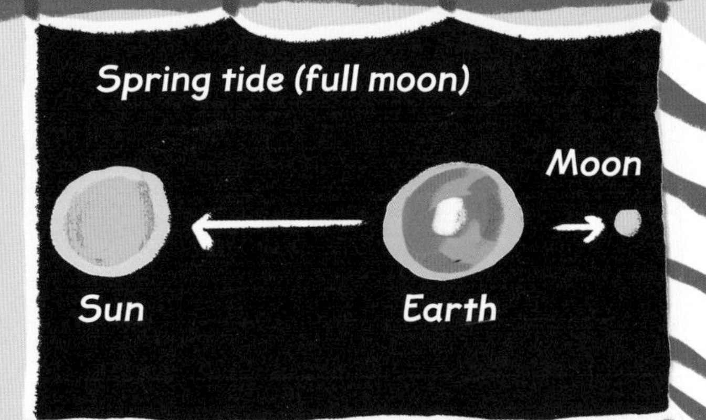

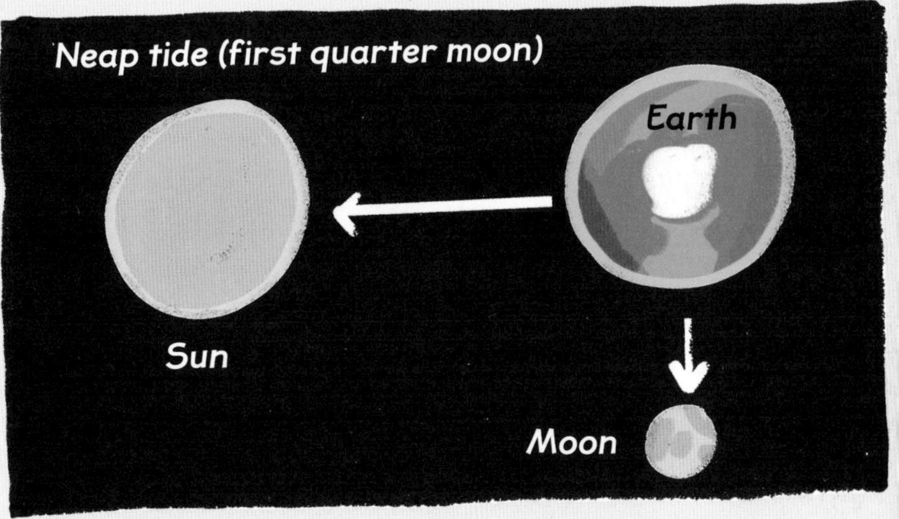

When the Sun and Moon are at right angles to each other, there are smaller tides than usual, called neap tides.

How did Apollo 11 get to the Moon?

In July 1969, three astronauts were launched on a huge Saturn V rocket. This carried them, inside a small spacecraft, into space, then on to the Moon.

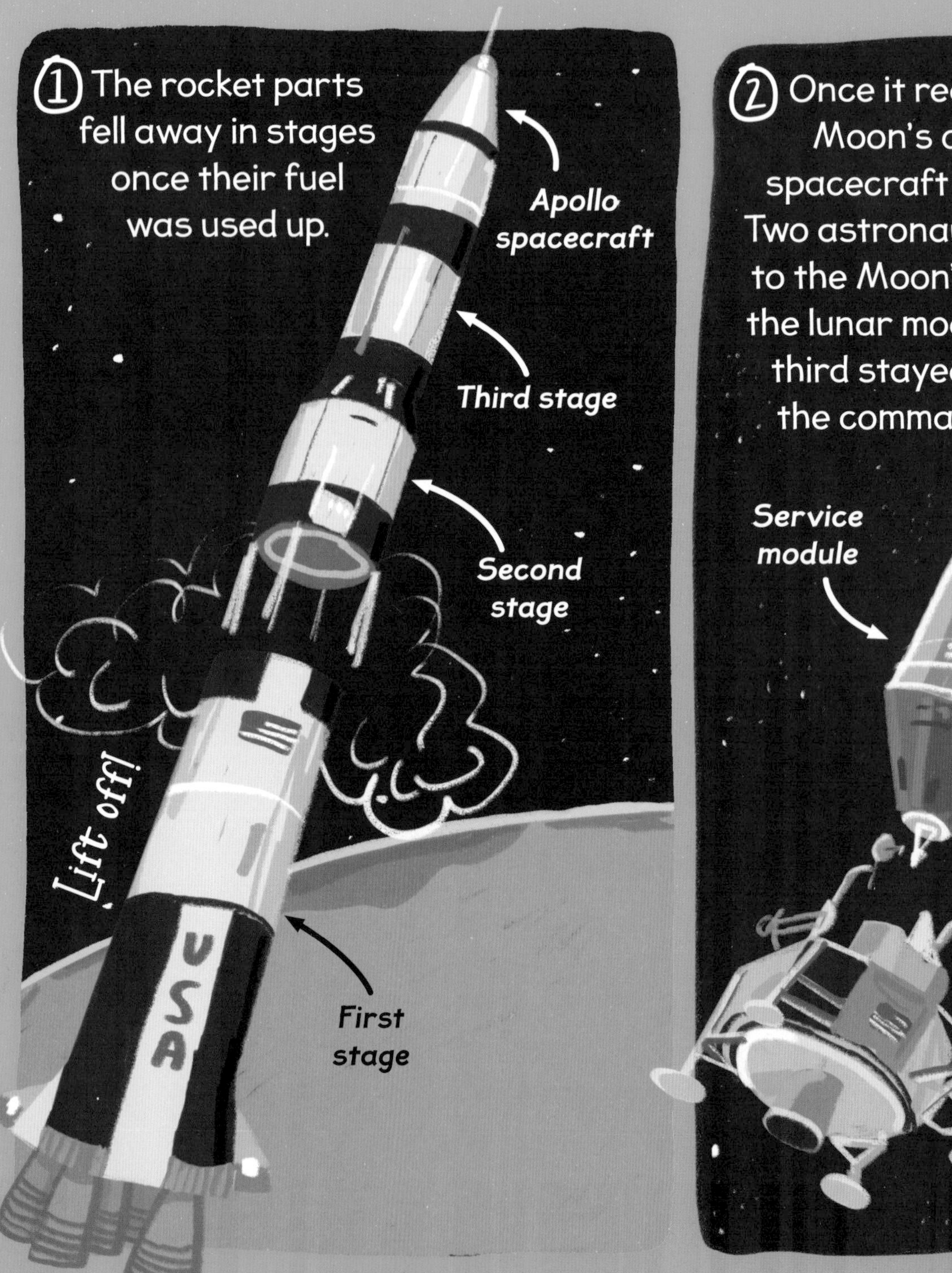

① The rocket parts fell away in stages once their fuel was used up.
Apollo spacecraft
Third stage
Second stage
First stage
USA
Lift off!

② Once it reached the Moon's orbit, the spacecraft separated. Two astronauts travelled to the Moon's surface in the lunar module, and the third stayed in orbit in the command module.
Service module
Command module
Lunar module

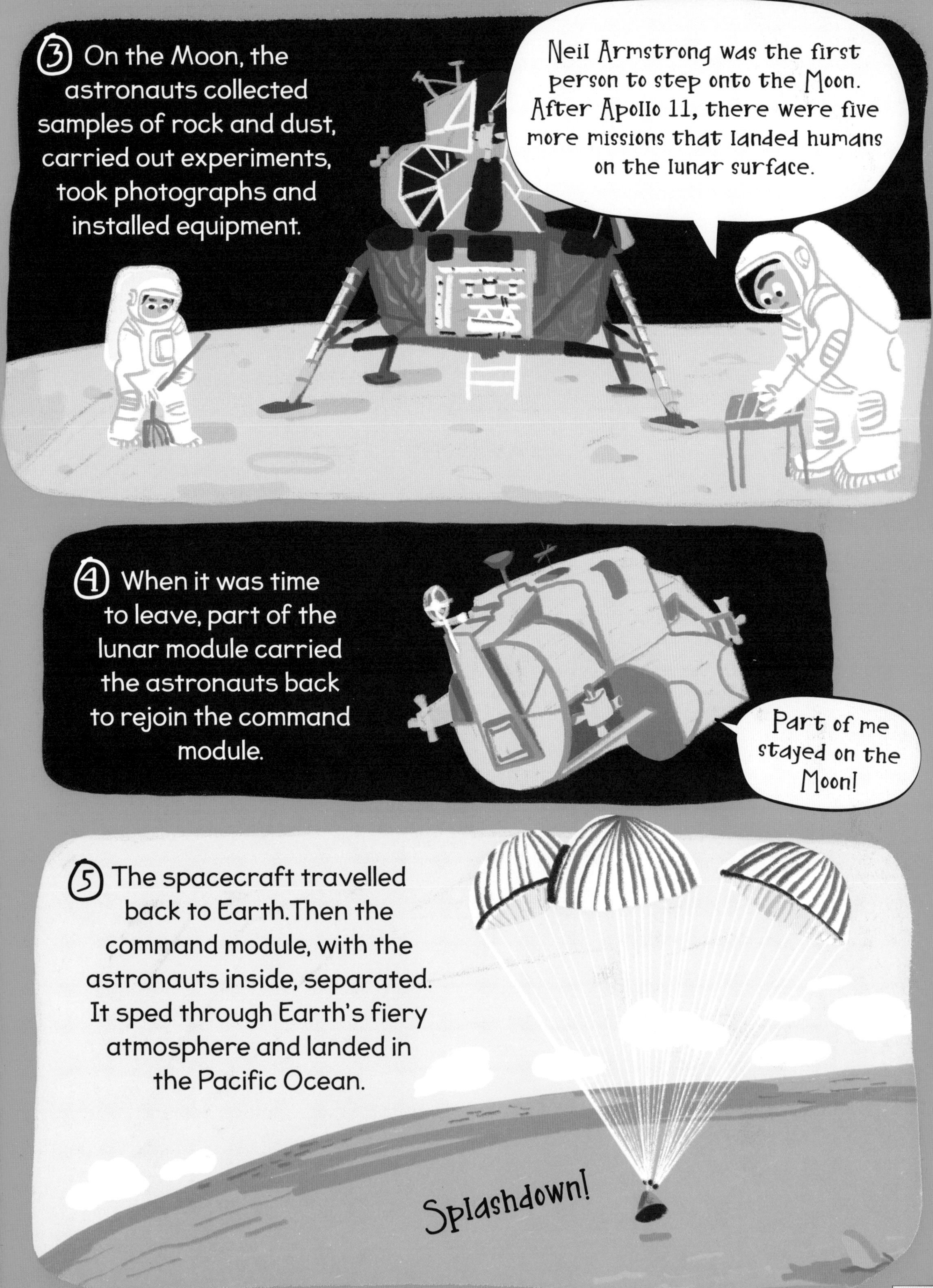

(3) On the Moon, the astronauts collected samples of rock and dust, carried out experiments, took photographs and installed equipment.
Neil Armstrong was the first person to step onto the Moon. After Apollo 11, there were five more missions that landed humans on the lunar surface.
(4) When it was time to leave, part of the lunar module carried the astronauts back to rejoin the command module.
Part of me stayed on the Moon!
(5) The spacecraft travelled back to Earth. Then the command module, with the astronauts inside, separated. It sped through Earth's fiery atmosphere and landed in the Pacific Ocean.
Splashdown!

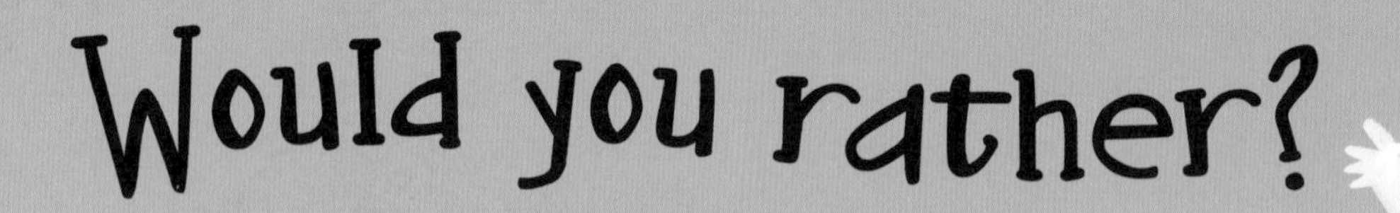

Would you rather visit the **far** side or the **near** side of the Moon?

Would you rather drive a **moon buggy** or be the **passenger**?

To leave your mark on the Moon, would you rather write your **name** in the regolith or leave a **photo** of yourself?

Each Apollo mission landed in a different place on the near side.

Would you rather visit the **Apollo sites** or go somewhere **unexplored**?

Would you prefer to climb **mountains**...

1
Would you rather be the first person on **Mars**, or the first to go back to the **Moon**?
Which would you bring back from the Moon: a **rock** or an **Apollo souvenir**?
Did you enjoy your journey?
Would you rather find aliens on the **Moon** or be visited by aliens on **Earth**?
It's time for lunar sports! Would you rather see how far you can **throw** a ball or see how high you can **jump**?
Would you rather fly the **orbiter** round and round the Moon, or guide the **lander** down to the surface?
...or explore **craters?**

Could we live on the Moon?

We could build a Moon base that would provide us with air to breathe and a place to grow food, and protect us from the extreme temperatures.

Outside the base, we have to wear spacesuits at all times and breathe air from a tank.

Is there any water?

There is no flowing water, but there is ice, which could be melted. It is underground in rocks, and in craters near the poles. The craters are always in shadow, so the lunar water stays frozen.

Water could even be used to make rocket fuel!

Why can't we breathe on the Moon?
The Moon doesn't have an atmosphere. It has a very thin layer of gases, called an exosphere. The mass of the exosphere is about 10 tonnes – the mass of two elephants. Earth's atmosphere has the mass of 10 quadrillion elephants!
Can I go to the Moon?
Not now – but if you become an astronaut when you grow up you might be able to. More Moon landings are planned, and we might build a lunar base to use as a stopping point on the way to Mars.

Which other planets have moons?

Mars has two but the other rocky planets, Mercury and Venus, don't have any. The gas giants, Jupiter and Saturn, and the ice giants, Uranus and Neptune, have lots – Saturn has at least 82!

Exoplanets – planets around other stars – probably have moons, too.
Earth
We're moonless!
Venus
Mercury
Mars
Jupiter
Are we all the same?

No, moons can be big or small. Some are icy and others are rocky. Some moons even have volcanoes that pour out ice or lava.

Why aren't all moons round?
Saturn
Moons come in many shapes – smaller moons are often not round. Gravity makes a moon round, but only if it's big enough.
Uranus
Some asteroids (rocks in space) have moons too!
Neptune

Does anything live on other moons?

We don't know. Some moons have a sea of liquid water under the surface – they might be home to tiny, simple forms of life.

A compendium of questions

How fast does the Moon travel?

It orbits Earth at 3683 kilometres an hour. It orbits the Sun at the same time, pulled along by Earth at 107,000 kilometres per hour.

Is it colder at the Moon's poles?

In places. The Sun is always on the horizon, and because of the Moon's uneven surface, some areas are always in sunlight and some are always cold.

Was the Moon the same when dinosaurs saw it?

The surface would have looked the same but it was closer, so looked bigger.

Light from the Sun makes me look yellow.

How did astronauts go to the toilet on the Moon landings?

They had to use a special bag each time, as there were no toilets on the spacecraft.

What colour is the Moon?

Grey. It looks white or yellow from Earth because it reflects a lot of light.

How do we know what the Moon is made of?

Scientists have examined rock and dust samples brought back by the Apollo missions.

Can I see Moon rocks?

There are moon rocks in museums around the world, so there might be one near you. Museums also have meteorites from the Moon – lumps that have been knocked off and have fallen to Earth.

Why can you sometimes see the Moon in the daytime?

As Earth turns, every place faces the Moon for some part of the 24-hour day. You are more likely to see the Moon in daytime when it's close to a full moon.

What can you hear on the Moon?

Nothing – there is no air to carry sounds. A falling rock wouldn't make a noise, and a rocket wouldn't roar as it took off.

Let's make some noise before we get to the Moon!

Could the Moon crash into Earth?

No. It would have to slow down enough to fall out of its orbit. Nothing could make it slow down that much.

NO ZOOM!

What's the one special object you'd take into space with you?
Would you rather walk on the Moon or photograph a planet?

What unique skill do you have that would make you a great astronaut?

ASTRONAUTS

Would you rather float about in space or speed around with a space pack?

What's the longest journey you've ever been on?

What is an astronaut?

An astronaut is a specially trained person who leaves Earth to travel into space. All around Earth, space stretches out between the distant planets and stars.

Astronauts are in here!
Moon
Rocket

Why do astronauts go into space?

To explore different places, such as the Moon, and to find out what it is like to live in space.

I am a cosmonaut, the Russian name for an astronaut.

How long do they spend in space?

Astronauts usually stay on the International Space Station (ISS) for six months, but four astronauts have spent over a year in space.

Most astronauts go to the ISS, which is 400 kilometres above Earth (less than the length of the UK). The furthest astronauts have been is to the Moon – 384,400 kilometres away.
Astronaut
International Space Station
Atmosphere
This is a layer of gases around Earth giving us air to breathe
Rocket launched from Earth
Earth

How do astronauts get into space?

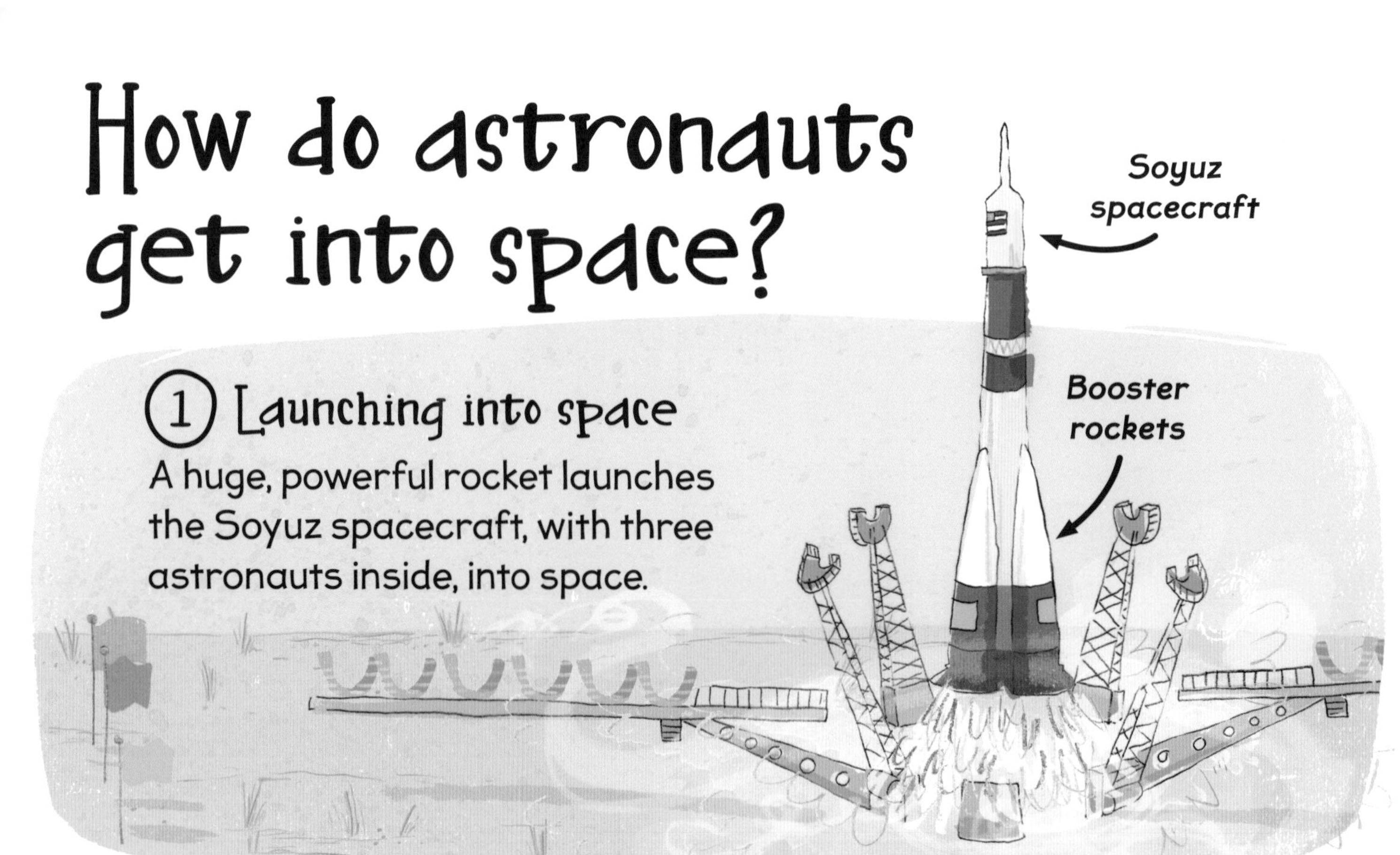

1 Launching into space

A huge, powerful rocket launches the Soyuz spacecraft, with three astronauts inside, into space.

2 Rocket separation

When the rocket is 50 kilometres up, its boosters separate. By the time it is 200 kilometres into space, the Soyuz spacecraft has separated from the rocket.

3 Circling Earth

The astronauts sit snugly in seats inside the spacecraft as it orbits Earth.

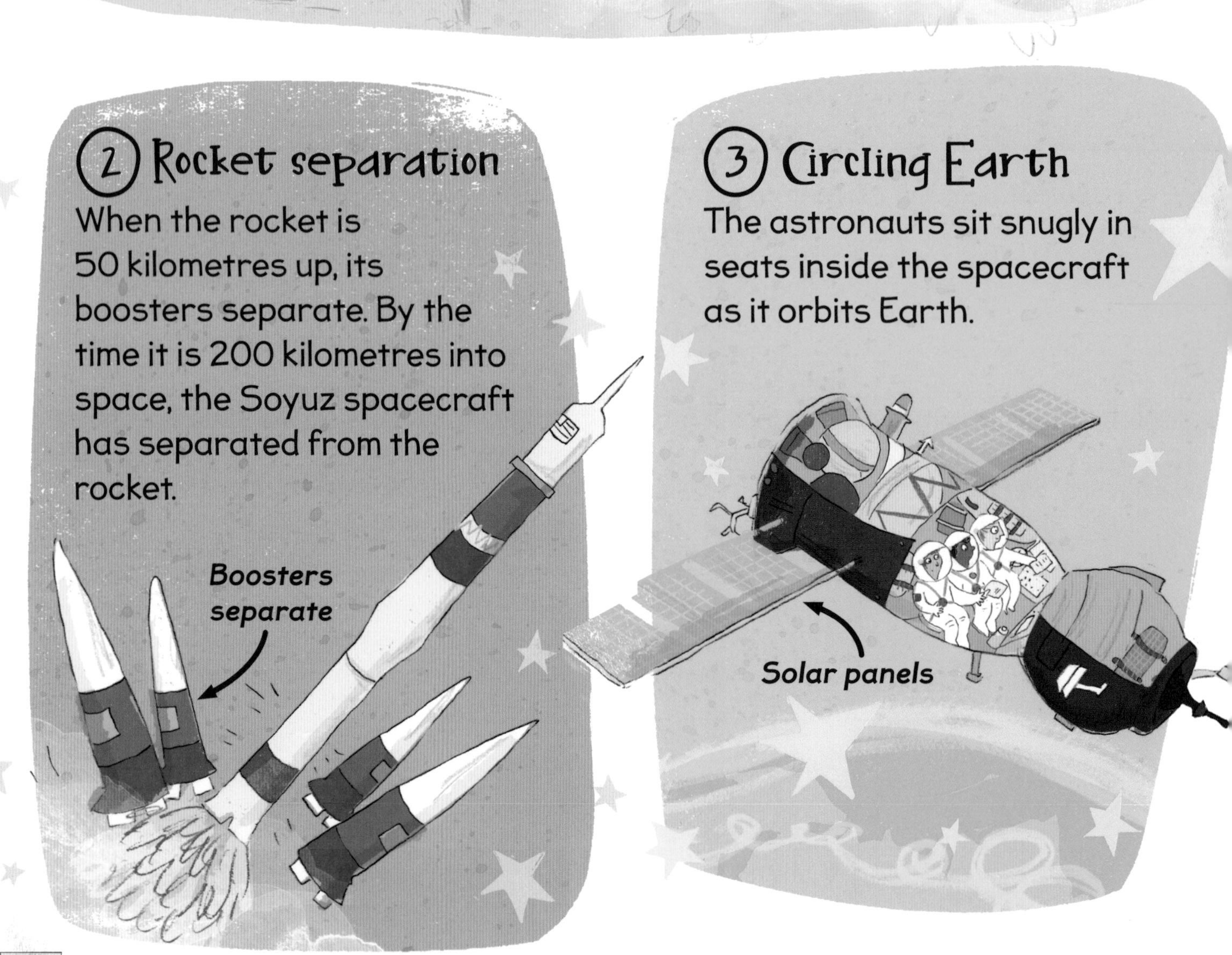

④ Docking

The spacecraft catches up with the ISS and locks onto it. The astronauts can then climb on board to meet the ISS crew.

⑤ Heading home

When the Soyuz spacecraft re-enters the air around Earth it is going extremely fast. The outside rubs against the air and gets incredibly hot, but the astronauts are safe inside. It's a bumpy ride though!

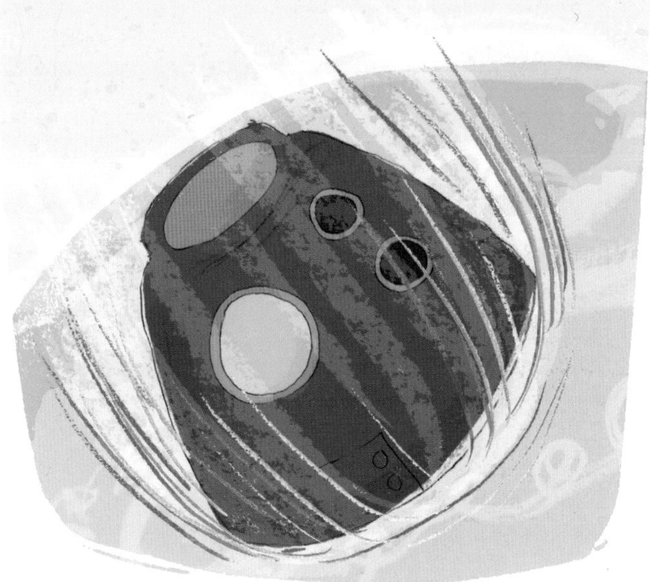

⑥ Safe landing

Astronauts feel nothing more than a bump when they land on the ground. They are helped onto recliners because their legs are weak after months of living in space.

Can anyone be an astronaut?

Any adult person who is fit and healthy can travel in space. Astronauts who go to the ISS have months of training, but in the future ordinary people will be able to go to space.

Now I know why they call this big plane the Vomit Comet – it makes me feel sick.

How do astronauts get used to floating in space?

In a big aeroplane flying in loops, trainee astronauts float for a short time as though they were weightless.

How do trainees practise spacewalks?

Wearing spacesuits underwater, they float in a huge tank. They can practise everything they will do when they go on spacewalks.

Vomit Comet
What special skills do they need?
Astronauts have to learn how everything on the space station works and how to fix it if it goes wrong. They also practise doing the experiments planned for their space trip.
Aspiring astronauts need to be very healthy because there are no hospitals in space. They also need to know about science or engineering.
Neutral Buoyancy Laboratory (underwater)

Did you know?

Astronauts built the **ISS**, joining the parts together in space.

Russian cosmonaut, Yuri Gagarin, was the **first person** to fly into space on 10 April 1961.

Between 1981 and 2011, American **space shuttles** carried astronauts into space. The shuttles flew many times, taking off like a rocket and landing back on a runway like a plane.

Spacewalking astronauts use a **tether** to fix themselves to the ISS so they can't float off.

You can sometimes see the ISS moving slowly across the sky like a **bright star** just after sunset.

Astronauts add **liquid** salt and pepper to their food. Grains or powder would float around and get into vital equipment.

The first person to walk on the **Moon** in July 1969 was Neil Armstrong.

Many astronauts get **space sick**, like travel sickness, but it soon wears off.

The first female astronaut, and the only **woman** to fly solo in space, was Valentina Tereshkova in 1963.

Peggy Whitson was the first **female commander** of the ISS in 2007 and 2016.

There have been **seven** astronaut tourists who have paid millions of dollars to fly to the ISS.

What do astronauts wear?

Inside a space station they wear ordinary clothes, but outside astronauts need a spacesuit to keep them alive. Spacesuits are very expensive – each costs about $12 million.

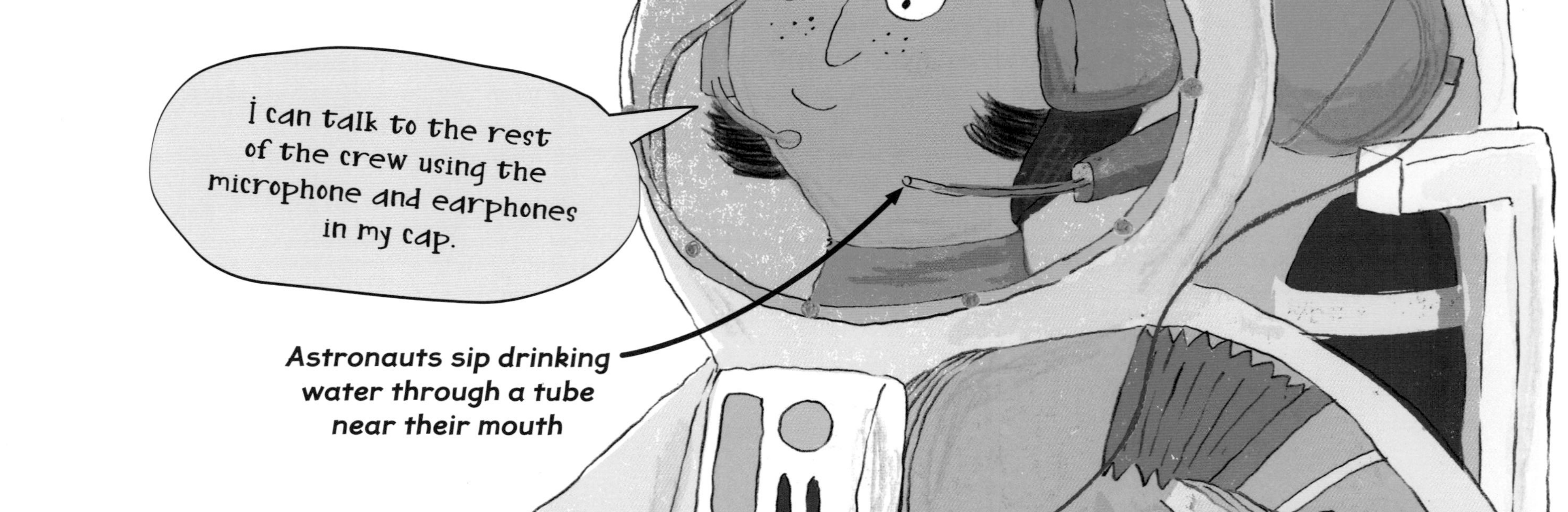

The helmet's gold visor protects the astronaut's eyes from the strong sunlight
A backpack, called a Life Support System, carries oxygen to breathe and water for cooling
I can talk to the rest of the crew using the microphone and earphones in my cap.
Astronauts sip drinking water through a tube near their mouth

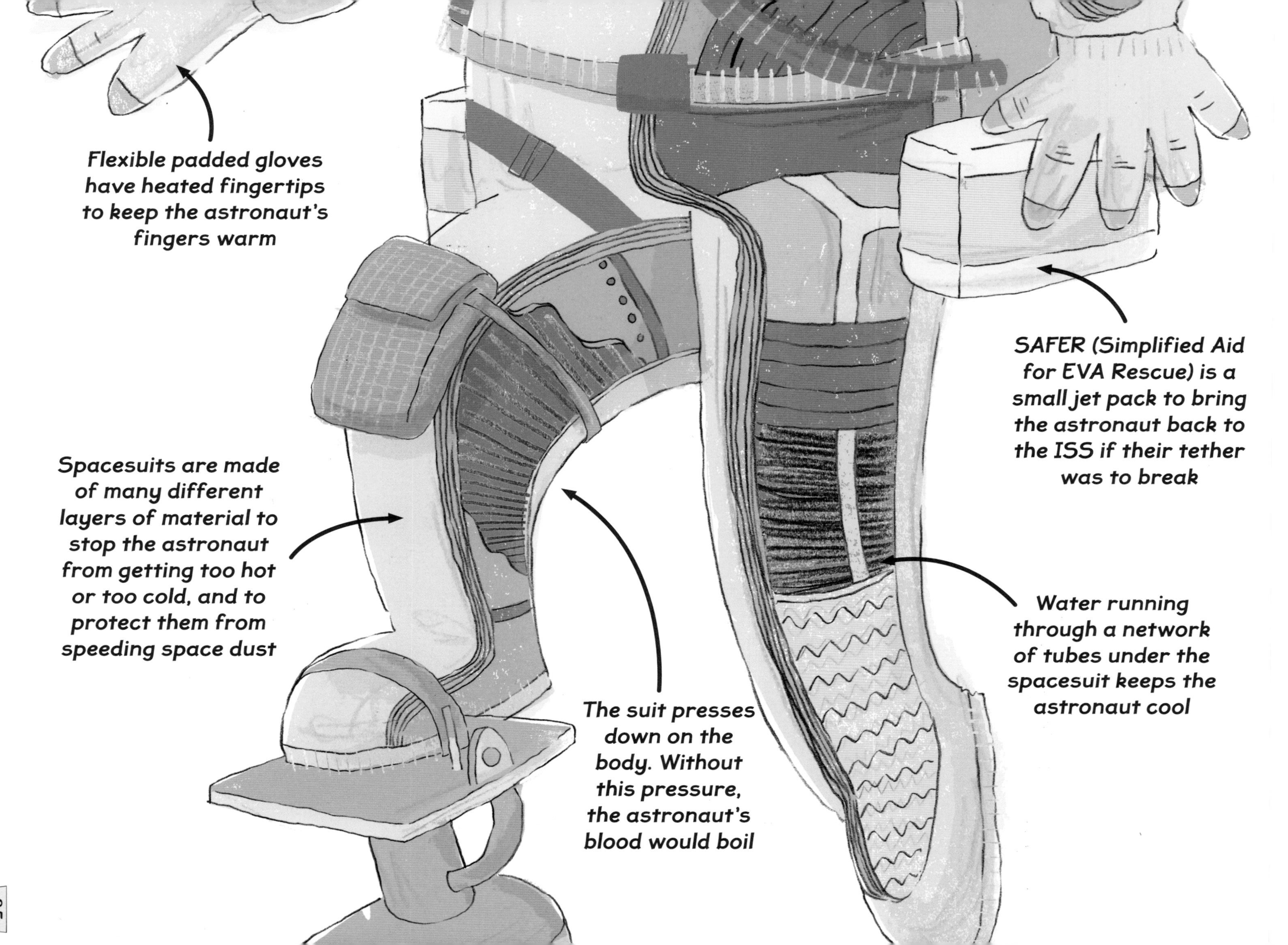
Flexible padded gloves have heated fingertips to keep the astronaut's fingers warm
Spacesuits are made of many different layers of material to stop the astronaut from getting too hot or too cold, and to protect them from speeding space dust
The suit presses down on the body. Without this pressure, the astronaut's blood would boil
SAFER (Simplified Aid for EVA Rescue) is a small jet pack to bring the astronaut back to the ISS if their tether was to break
Water running through a network of tubes under the spacesuit keeps the astronaut cool

Where do astronauts live?

The International Space Station, which is circling the Earth, is home to astronauts exploring space. It is made of sections called modules where astronauts can eat, sleep and work.

Does everything float in a space station?

Yes! On Earth, gravity pulls everything down to the ground, but in a space station, the astronauts and everything else like food, water and tools float around if they are not fixed down. We say they are weightless.

Docking area

International Space Station

How do astronauts get food and water?

Everything they need is delivered from Earth in a Soyuz spacecraft or a robot ferry.

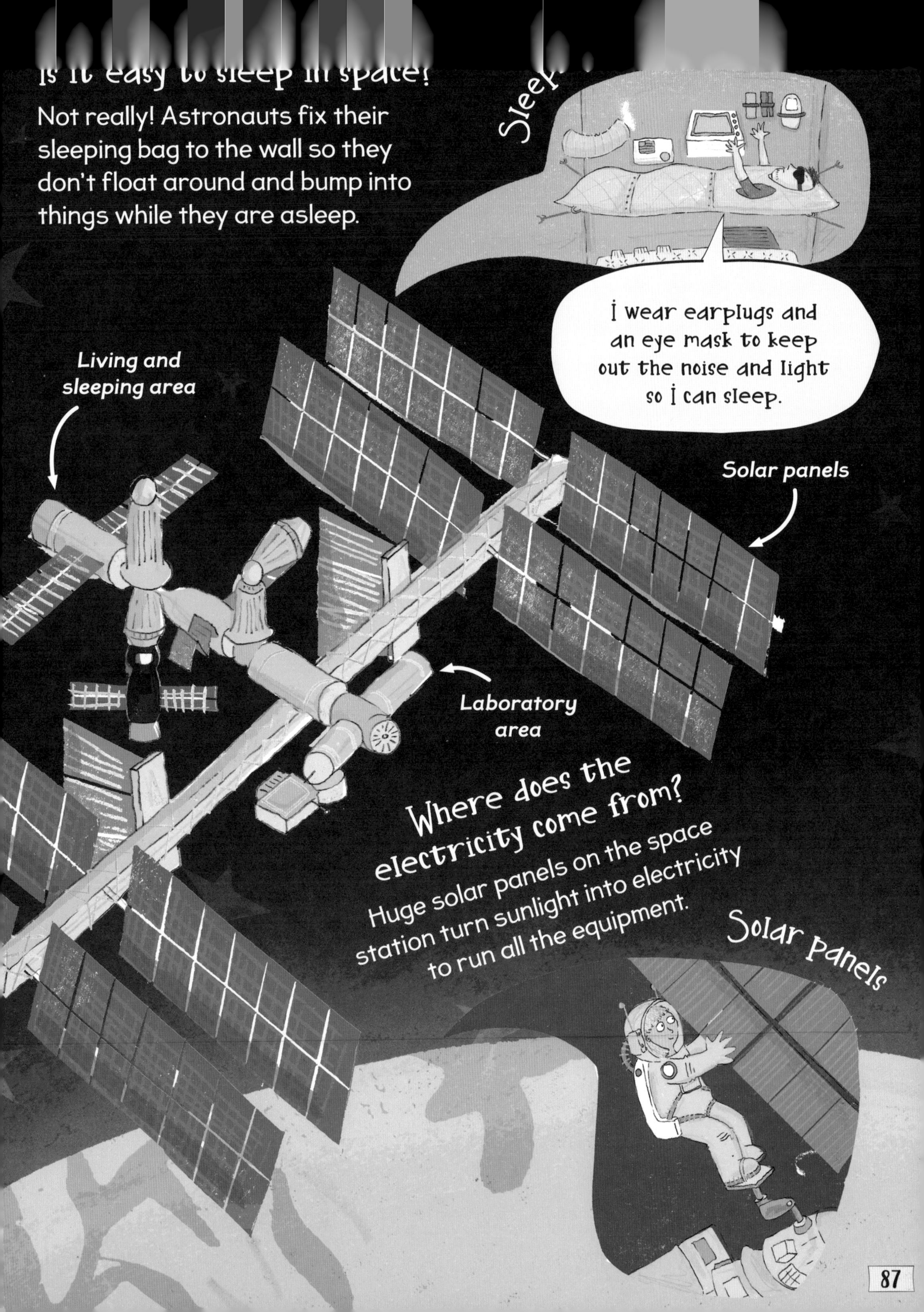
I wear earplugs and an eye mask to keep out the noise and light so I can sleep.
Living and sleeping area
Solar panels
Laboratory area
Solar panels

Is it easy to sleep in space?

Not really! Astronauts fix their sleeping bag to the wall so they don't float around and bump into things while they are asleep.

Where does the electricity come from?

Huge solar panels on the space station turn sunlight into electricity to run all the equipment.

How many?

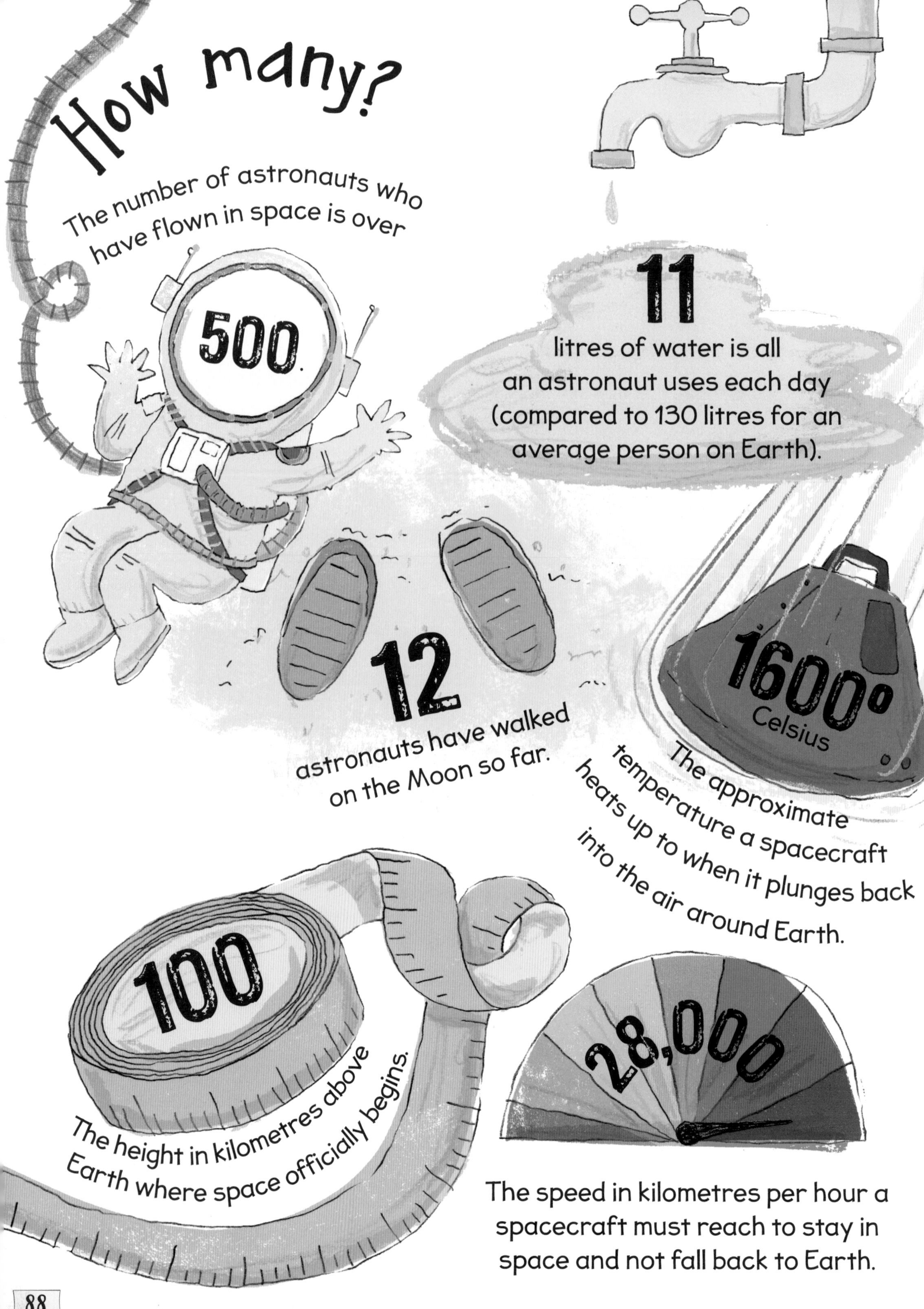
The number of astronauts who have flown in space is over
500.
11
litres of water is all an astronaut uses each day (compared to 130 litres for an average person on Earth).
12
astronauts have walked on the Moon so far.
1600°
Celsius
The approximate temperature a spacecraft heats up to when it plunges back into the air around Earth.
100
The height in kilometres above Earth where space officially begins.
28,000
The speed in kilometres per hour a spacecraft must reach to stay in space and not fall back to Earth.

The ISS has a supply of about **2400** litres of water but over 90 percent of it, including toilet water and sweat, is recycled!

Astronauts from **18** different countries have lived on the ISS.

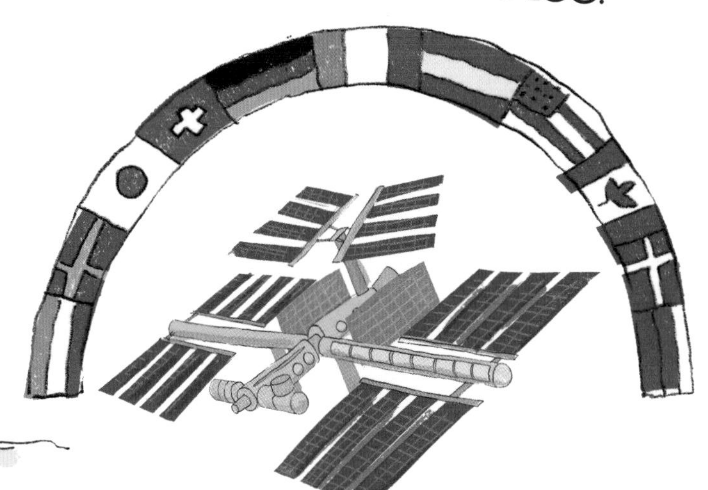

The oldest astronaut so far is John Glenn. He went into space at the age of **77**.

3 The number of days it took the Apollo astronauts to get to the Moon.

A spacesuit back pack provides an astronaut with about **8.5** hours of oxygen and water, and enough nitrogen gas for the SAFER jet thrusters to power back to the ISS.

What do astronauts eat?

They eat the same as you, but choose their favourite foods before they go. The food is cooked on Earth and then sent to the space station in ready-to-eat portions.

Food is dried so it lasts longer and is lighter for the journey.

Adding hot water to this packet of dried food makes it into a tasty meal. The packet is fixed to my tray to stop it floating away.

Spaghetti

Cups are no good to us, because drinks float out of them. We add water to a packet of dried powder then suck the drink through a straw.

We've just had a delivery of fresh fruit from Earth. We'll have to eat it quickly because we don't have a fridge to keep it fresh.
Orange
Apple
We don't eat crumbly foods like bread because the crumbs float around and get stuck in equipment.
Beef and mashed potato
Chicken and rice
Flapjack

Why do astronauts exercise in space?

Exercise helps to keep the astronauts strong and healthy. Their bodies change in space without gravity to pull them down to the ground. They get taller, and their bones and muscles get weaker.

My space exercise bike doesn't have a saddle. A harness keeps me in place and my feet clip onto the pedals.

How much exercise do they do?

Two hours of exercise every day is enough to keep an astronaut's heart and muscles strong.

Weightlifting in space doesn't build up muscle because the weights feel as light as a feather! Instead we pull or push against strong springs.
British astronaut Tim Peake ran 42 kilometres, the same distance as the London marathon, on a treadmill in the ISS in April 2016.
Couldn't they just run around the ISS?
No, astronauts need straps to hold them down to each piece of equipment and provide resistance for their muscles.
Do they come home looking different?
Astronauts can get up to five centimetres taller because the bones in their backs stretch apart without gravity pulling them together. Weightlessness can also make their faces look puffy.

What jobs are done in space?

We monitor our bodies to see how we cope with weightlessness.

Astronauts are very busy. They look after the ISS, keep it clean and tidy, and repair anything that goes wrong. They also do lots of experiments.

Who cleans the ISS?

Everyone helps to clean once a week. Astronauts use a vacuum cleaner to remove dust. They also check everything is working well and fix it if not.

I'm using wipes and a cloth sprayed with detergent to remove any dirt.

One day we may be able to grow most of our own food in space.

What experiments do astronauts do?

They try to find out how things, such as crystals and plants, grow differently in space.

What is an EVA?

Extra Vehicular Activity (EVA) is the name for a spacewalk. This is when astronauts put on spacesuits to work outside the space station, installing new equipment or doing repairs.

Do astronauts have robot helpers?

Yes! Canadarm2 is a robot arm on the outside of the ISS. Astronauts operate it from inside, and it can help to move or install bulky parts.

Why do astronauts take living things into space?

They study how things behave differently in space. They grow seeds, as well as watch insects and small animals to study how quickly they get used to weightlessness.

Would you rather?

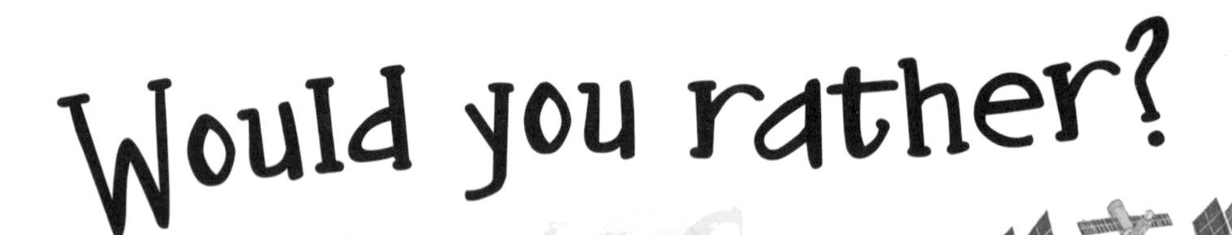

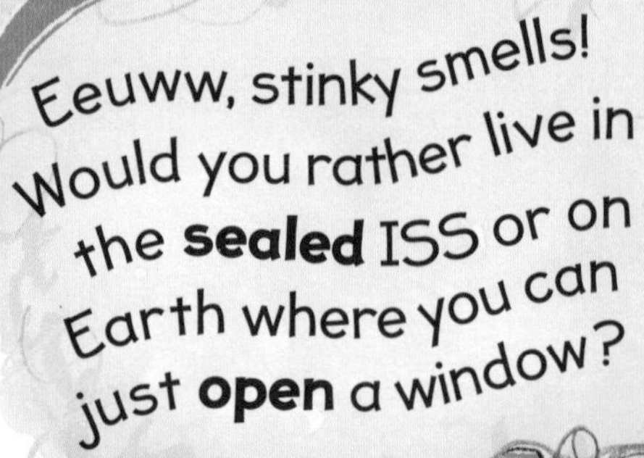

Eeuww, stinky smells! Would you rather live in the **sealed** ISS or on Earth where you can just **open** a window?

Would you rather **live** in a space station circling Earth or **travel** for six months to visit Mars?

If you were working in space, would you prefer to **suit up** for a space walk outside or stay inside in **pyjamas** to operate a robot arm?

Time for pooping practice! Would you prefer a **comfy toilet** at home or aiming at a teeny hole on a **space toilet**?

Would you rather watch spiders **spin webs** or ants **build tunnels** in weightlessness?
Would you prefer to float inside a **space station** or float around a **swimming pool** on Earth?
Would you rather play **golf** on the Moon (like astronaut Alan Shephard in 1971) or **table tennis** on the ISS?
Would you prefer to look down at **Earth** from the ISS or stare at the **Moon** from Earth through a telescope?

Can astronauts take a bath?

Astronauts don't bath in space, because water would not run out of a tap or stay in a bath. Water turns into balls of liquid that float around.

To wash my hair I rub shampoo and a little water into it, then use a comb and towel to remove the dirt.

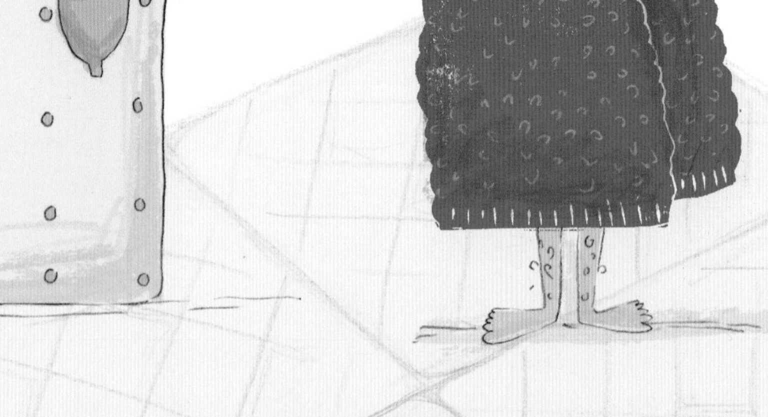

Instead of taking a shower, I have washed myself with a soapy cloth and am now towelling dry.

How about having a shower instead?

The US Skylab space station in 1973 did have a shower. It was sealed shut to keep all the water inside and the astronauts had to vacuum up the water before they could get out.

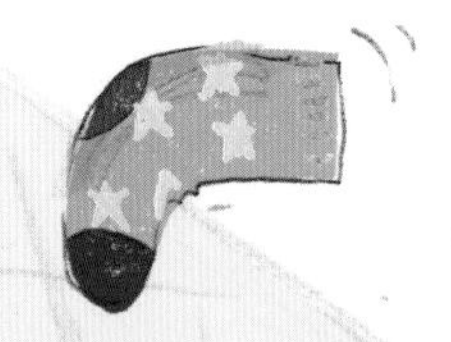

How do they brush their teeth?

I clean my teeth with an ordinary toothbrush, but use special toothpaste that I can swallow. There's no need to rinse with water.

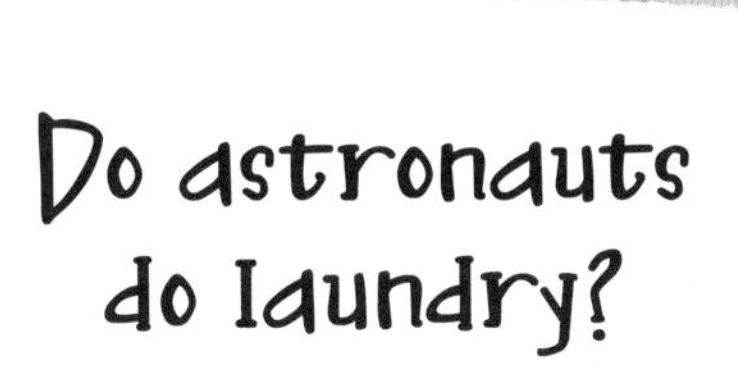

Do astronauts do laundry?

Astronauts save water by not washing their clothes. They throw away their underwear and socks, but keep wearing the same outer clothes for about six weeks!

Where does their poo go?

Space toilets do not use water for flushing. Flowing air sucks the waste away into bags to be recycled or taken back to Earth. Astronauts have to fix themselves down so they stay on the toilet.

Will people ever visit Mars?

Yes, there are plans to send people to Mars. The journey will take six months each way. They will have to take everything they need to stay alive – food, water and air to breathe.

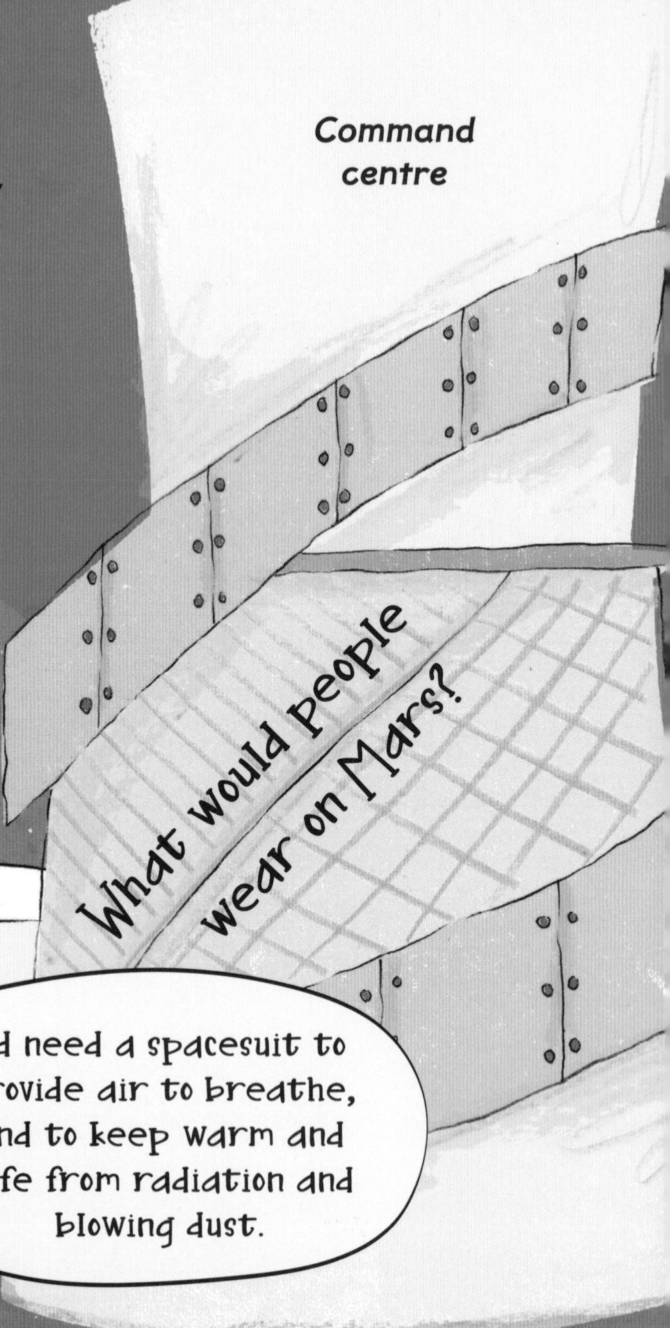

Command centre

What would people wear on Mars?

I'd need a spacesuit to provide air to breathe, and to keep warm and safe from radiation and blowing dust.

Laboratory

Is there any water to drink?

There is no running water on Mars, but there is frozen ice that could be used near its north and south poles.

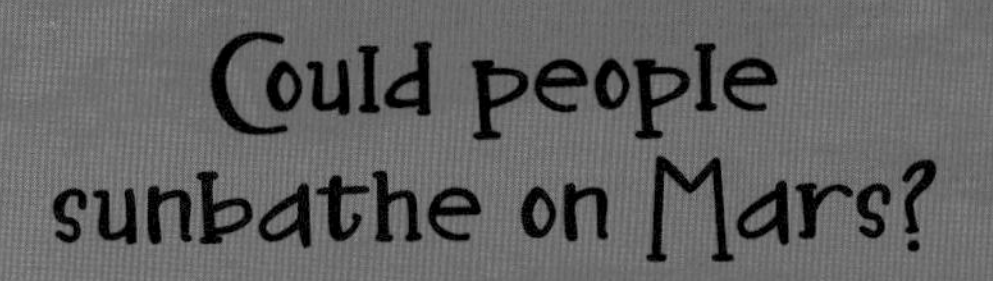

Could people sunbathe on Mars?

It would be far too cold! Mars is further from the Sun than Earth. It's also dry and windy, and there are often huge dust storms.

Dust storm

Is the air on Mars breathable?

No. Humans need oxygen gas to breathe and the air on Mars is mostly carbon dioxide gas.

Where could they live?

If astronauts built homes on Mars, they would need thick walls to protect against dangerous radiation. They might even build homes underground.

A compendium of questions

How often do astronauts see a sunrise?

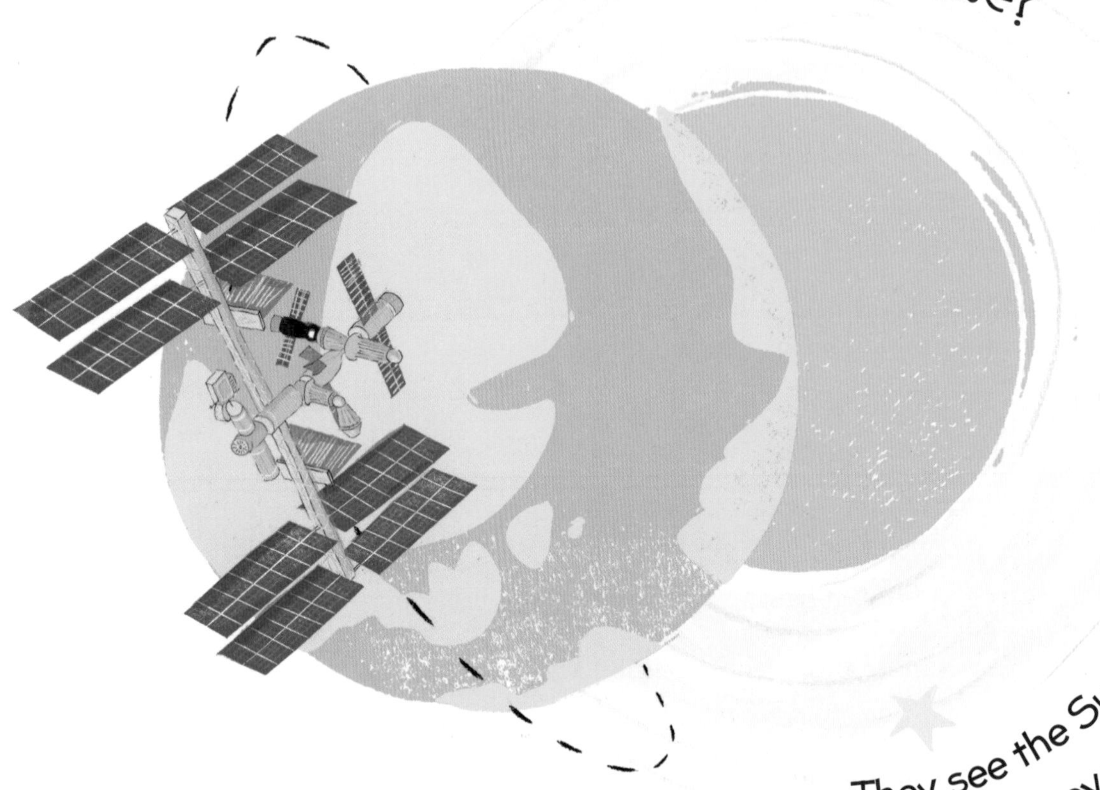

They see the Sun rise and set 16 times every day from the ISS as it circles Earth.

We have a full house today!

How many astronauts live on the ISS?

Usually six, but there are nine when a new crew arrives.

How big is the ISS?

The living space inside is bigger than a six-bedroom house. The whole station stretches out to about the size of a sports field.

How fast does the ISS travel?

27,600 kilometres per hour, about 30 times faster than a Boeing 747 jet.

Ewww! Let's get rid of this fast!

What happens to waste and rubbish?

They seal it in bags and put it in a cargo spacecraft, which either lands on Earth or burns up in the air.

Why do astronauts like spicy food?

Weightlessness can give astronauts stuffy noses, so stronger flavours taste better.

Who was Laika?

A dog – and the first living creature to orbit Earth in 1957.

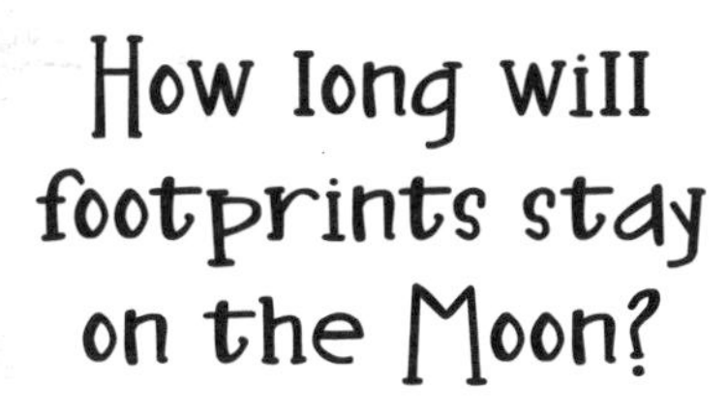

How long will footprints stay on the Moon?

Millions of years because there is no air on the Moon to blow them away.

When did the first astronauts go to the ISS?

In 2000 and there have been astronauts on board ever since.

Which countries have launched astronauts with their own rockets?

China, Russia and USA. Astronauts from other countries travel on US or Russian rockets.

Who would you take with you on a trip to the International Space Station?
What's your favourite space machine?

Would you prefer to walk or drive a buggy on the Moon?

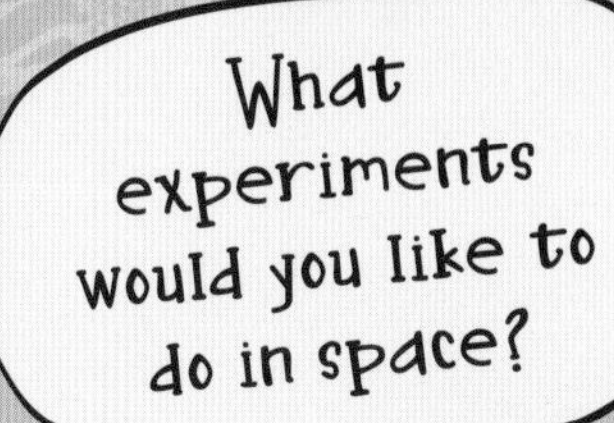

What experiments would you like to do in space?

SPACE MACHINES

Would you rather orbit the Moon or Mars?

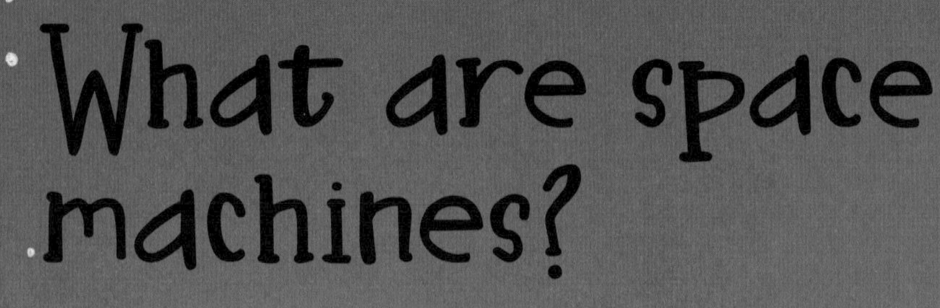

What are space machines?

Any machines that are sent into space! They include rockets, shuttles, satellites and probes.

I travel around (orbit) Earth and keep track of the weather.
Meteosat weather satellite
Hubble Space Telescope
Falcon 9 rocket
I've been succeeded by the James Webb Space Telescope!
Space starts 80–100 kilometres above Earth's sea level.

I blast spacecraft from Earth into space.
Lunar Reconnaissance Orbiter
I'm in orbit around the Moon right now!
International Space Station
I'm a large base in space where astronauts live and work.
I was the size of a beach ball!

Do space machines come back to Earth?

A few come back to Earth after their missions, while others carry on working in space. Some are deliberately crashed into a moon or planet, or left behind there. The rest end up as 'space junk'.

Which was the first space machine?

The Russian satellite Sputnik was launched in 1957 and was the first satellite to orbit Earth. Sputnik started a 'space race' between Soviet Russia and the USA. The two countries competed to see who could achieve the most in space.

Which was the biggest rocket?

The Saturn V rockets used to carry the Apollo spacecraft to the Moon were the largest rockets that have ever launched.

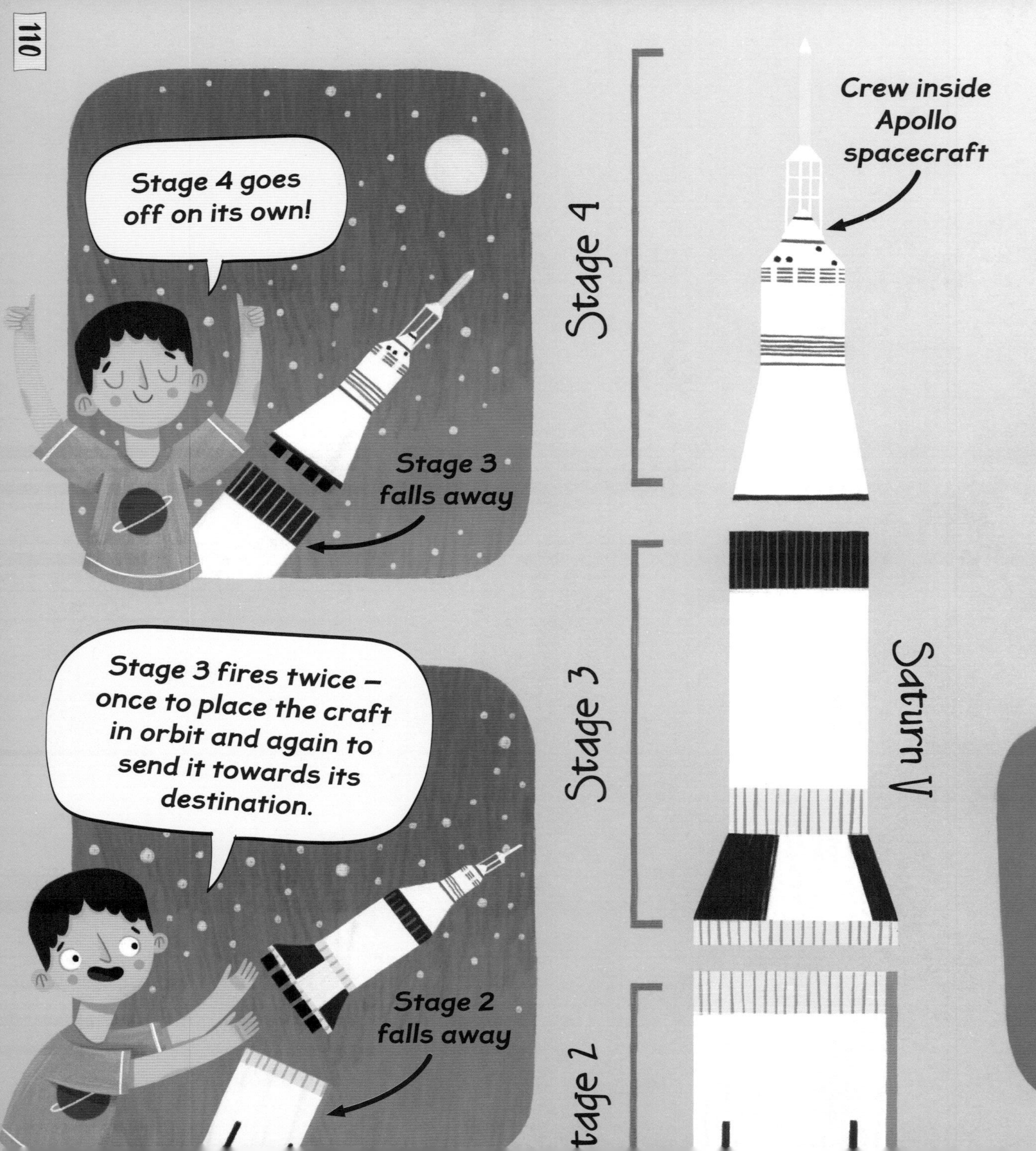
Stage 4 goes off on its own!
Stage 3 falls away
Stage 3 fires twice – once to place the craft in orbit and again to send it towards its destination.
Stage 2 falls away
Stage 4
Stage 3
tage 2
Crew inside Apollo spacecraft
Saturn V

How do rockets take off?

At launch, rockets stand upright. They burn huge amounts of liquid or solid fuel, which makes a lot of exhaust. This blasts out of the back of the rocket, pushing it upwards.

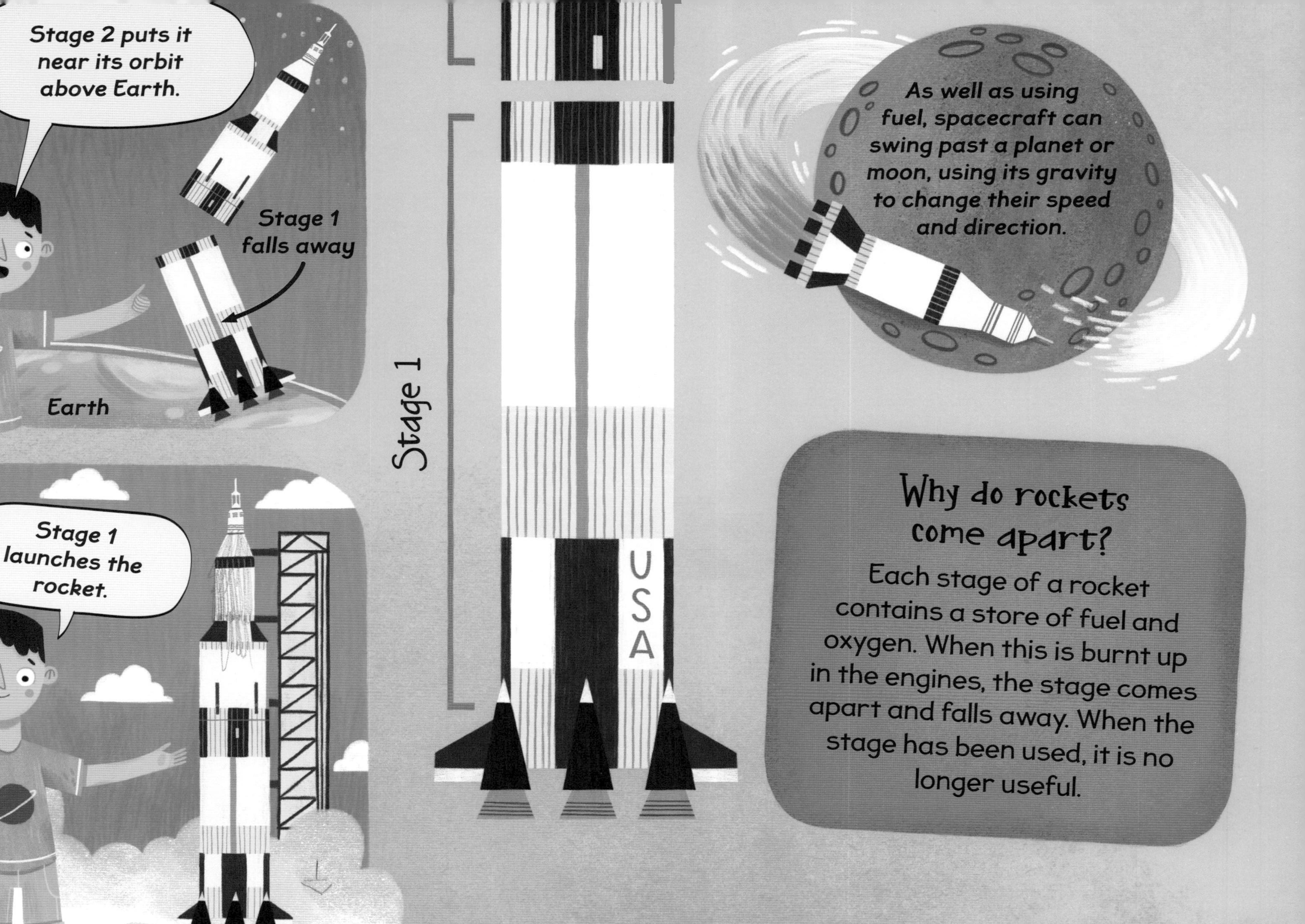

Stage 2 puts it near its orbit above Earth.
Stage 1 falls away
Earth
Stage 1 launches the rocket.
Stage 1
USA
As well as using fuel, spacecraft can swing past a planet or moon, using its gravity to change their speed and direction.

Why do rockets come apart?

Each stage of a rocket contains a store of fuel and oxygen. When this is burnt up in the engines, the stage comes apart and falls away. When the stage has been used, it is no longer useful.

Who was the first person in space?

In 1961, Russian Yuri Gagarin travelled into space in Vostok 1 – a tiny capsule launched by a rocket. It circled Earth once, taking 89 minutes, then came back down. Gagarin left the craft with a parachute.

Cosmonaut Yuri Gagarin.

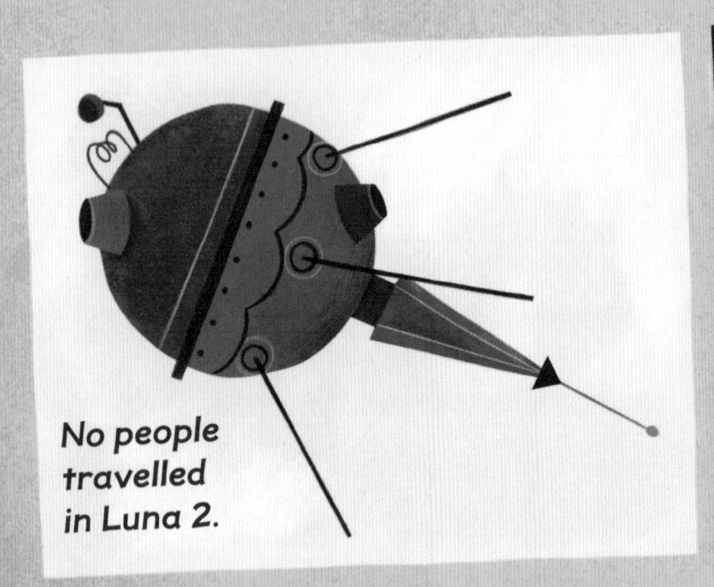

No people travelled in Luna 2.

Which spacecraft landed on the Moon first?

The Russian Luna 2 in 1959. Lots of spacecraft have been to the Moon since then, including six American Apollo craft carrying astronauts.

How did Apollo land on the Moon?

After being launched by a Saturn V rocket, the Apollo spacecraft was pulled into orbit by the Moon's gravity. A lander then separated and went down to the Moon's surface.

The service and command module stayed in space.

Who was first to walk on the Moon?

Me! I'm an American astronaut called Neil Armstrong.
And I was next. I'm Buzz Aldrin. We went together on Apollo 11 in 1969.
I'm Michael Collins. I stayed in the command module.

When the astronauts were ready to leave the Moon, thrusters blasted part of the lander back up into space to rejoin the service and command module.

This is much easier than walking!

The Moon buggy could drive over objects up to 30 centimetres high.

Did the astronauts have a car on the Moon?

Kind of! The last three Apollo missions in 1971 and 1972 took a Moon buggy to drive on the surface.

How many?

2.5 million

The number of parts in a space shuttle.

40,300

The speed in kilometres per hour a rocket needs to reach to leave Earth's atmosphere.

5

space shuttles were built and flew into space many times. There were **135** flights.

There are **8** layers in the Extravehicular Mobility Unit worn for spacewalks.

1 million

The number of people the technology company SpaceX hope to have living on Mars in 100 years.

1323

The total number of flight-days of the five NASA space shuttles over 30 years.

924,675
The number of litres of fuel used by the first stage of a Saturn V rocket.

10
space stations have successfully launched and been occupied.

0.14 The top speed in kilometres per hour of the Curiosity Mars rover.

18
The top speed in kilometres per hour of the Moon buggy.

There are **128 million** pieces of space junk one millimetre to one centimetre wide orbiting Earth right now.

Only **1** space station is still operational.

How are satellites placed in space?

The Moon

I'm Earth's only natural satellite!

Rockets and space shuttles have carried satellites into space. A rocket carries the satellite to the right height, then fires smaller rockets to adjust its position and release the satellite.

Why don't they float off into space?

Satellites are held in place by Earth's gravity. They use thrusters to stay up as they start to slip towards Earth over time.

What are they used for?
Lots of things! Some satellites track the weather or your location, while others bounce radio waves around Earth to provide TV, radio and internet signals.
Weather satellite
Communications satellite
How big are they?
The smallest are CubeSats, which are just a few centimetres across and weigh less than an apple! The largest satellite is as big as a football field.

Would you rather?

Be the **first** human on **Mars**...
...or **first** to find a desert **island**?
Would you rather **discover** a new **planet** with a telescope...
...or **visit** the **Moon**?
What's better? A **holiday** on the International Space Station or **climbing** Mount Everest?

Would you prefer to invent a **spaceship** that could travel to Jupiter in one day...
...or a **flying car**?
SAM
SAM
Would you rather have a **rocket** or a **satellite** named after you?
Who would you like to **meet** more, an **alien**...
...or your favourite **movie star**?
Would you prefer to spend a day in **zero gravity**...
...or seeing **great white sharks** in the wild?
What's better? Going on a **spacewalk** or controlling the **space station**?

What is the International Space Station?

It's a research base in space. Built from modules arranged along a solid metal backbone, it is powered by solar panels. Astronauts live there for six months at a time.

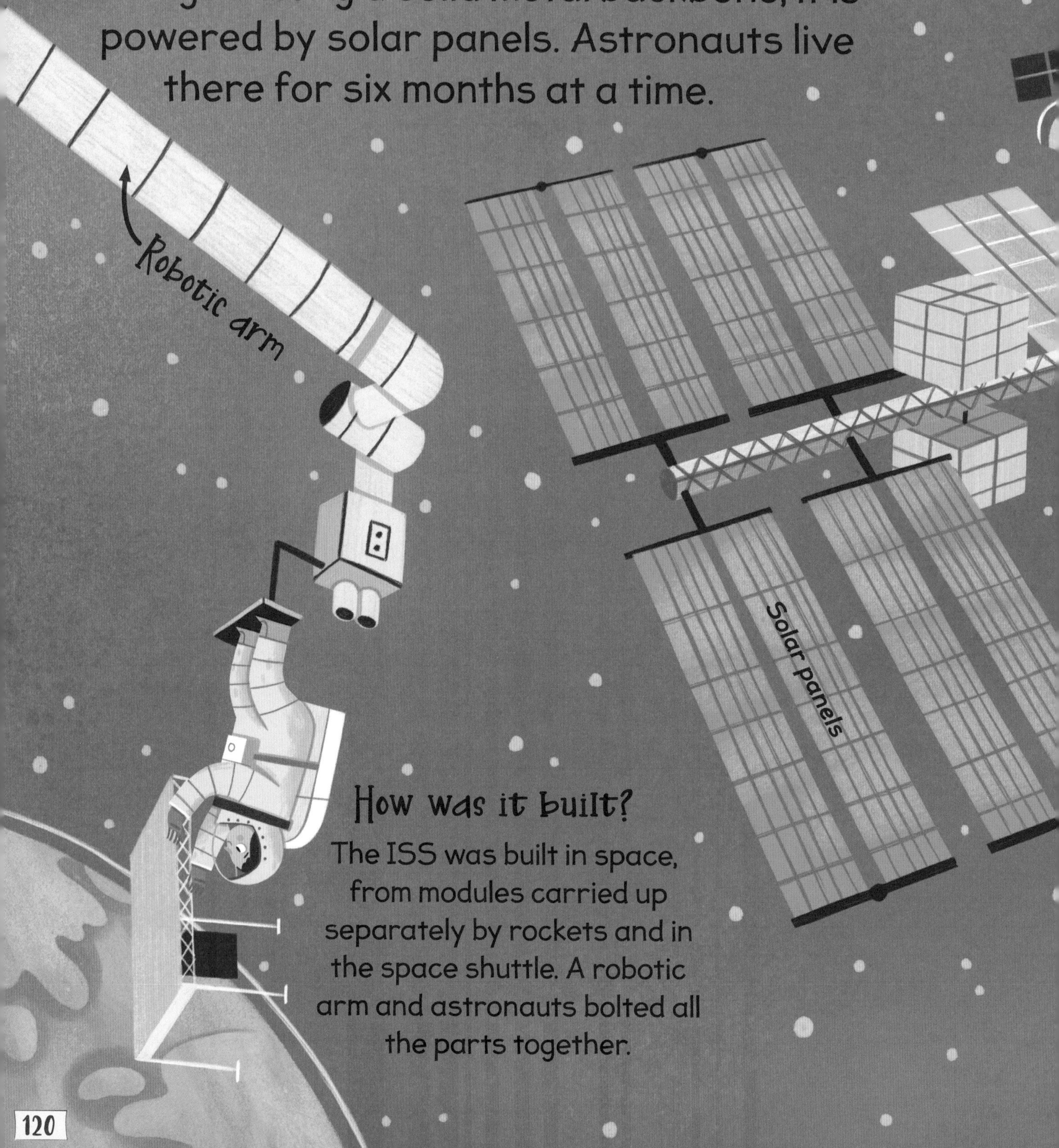

Robotic arm

Solar panels

How was it built?

The ISS was built in space, from modules carried up separately by rockets and in the space shuttle. A robotic arm and astronauts bolted all the parts together.

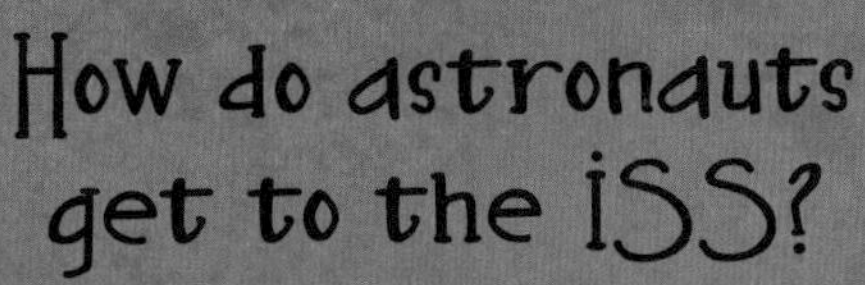

How do astronauts get to the ISS?

International Space Station (ISS)

At first they were carried by a space shuttle, which went to the ISS and came back to Earth. Now they go in a Russian Soyuz craft and return in its descent module.

Space shuttle

Is the ISS speedy?

Yes! The ISS travels at 8 kilometres per second at a height of 360 kilometres. It covers a distance equivalent to the Moon and back every day!

What's life like on board?

It's not easy! There is zero gravity, so the crew float about. This makes eating, drinking, washing and going to the toilet more difficult!

Every day is a bad hair day in space!

What is an EMU?

The EMU (Extravehicular Mobility Unit) is like a mini spacecraft worn by astronauts. It allows them to go on spacewalks outside their spacecraft. The EMU has a life support system and a jetpack.

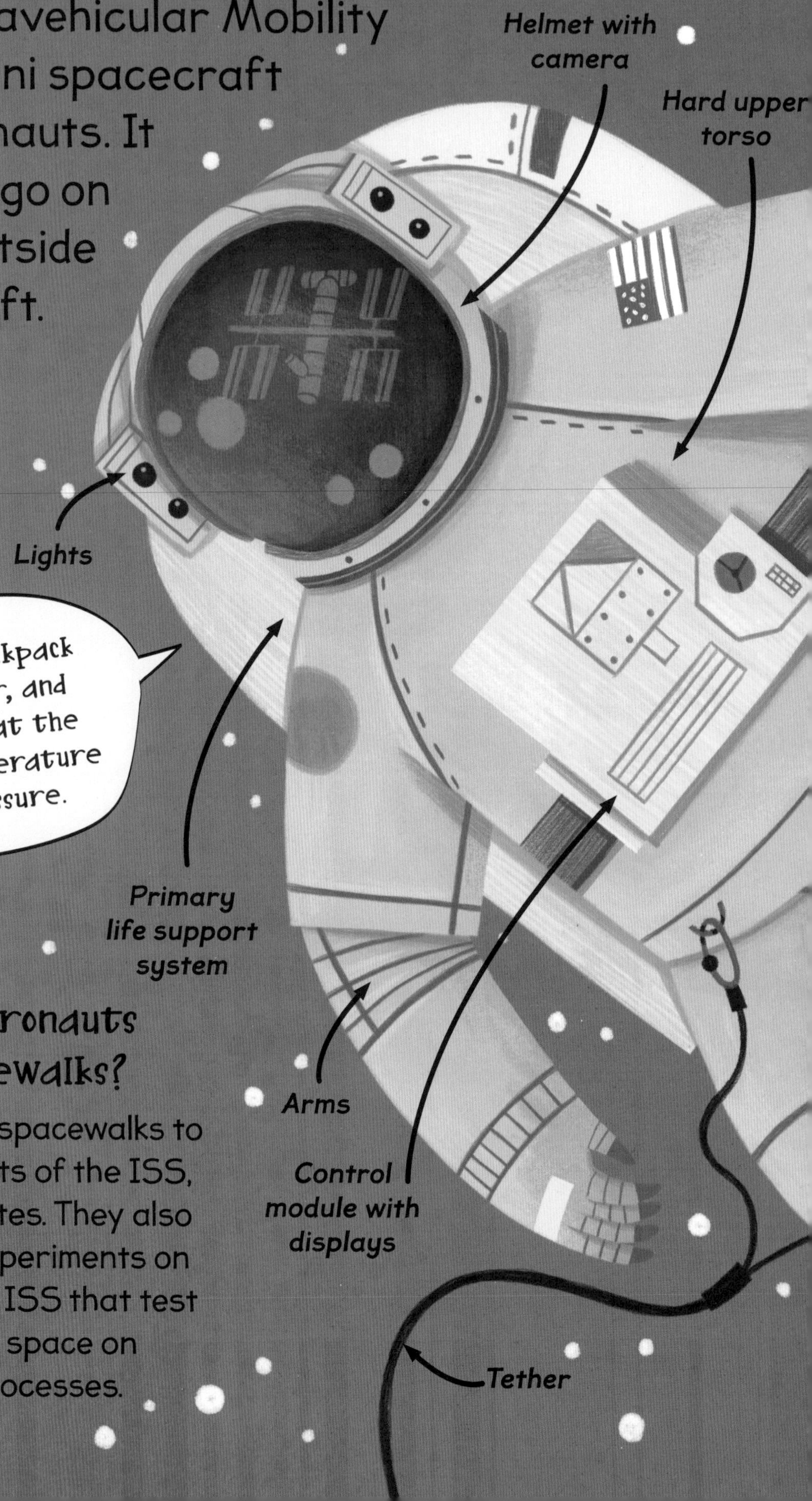

Why do astronauts go on spacewalks?

Astronauts go on spacewalks to fix or change parts of the ISS, or to mend satellites. They also place or check experiments on the outside of the ISS that test the effects of space on objects or processes.

Why don't astronauts float away?

Astronauts attach their tether to different parts of the spacecraft so they stay tethered as they move. They can also use the rescue module of their EMU backpack, which has 24 jet thrusters to move them around.

What is the robotic arm used for?

The ISS has a hinged 'arm' with a 'hand' at each end. One end grabs onto the space station while the other end carries astronauts, moves equipment and secures docking spacecraft.

What are space probes?

Probes are unmanned robotic spacecraft. They go on long journeys to explore objects in space, including planets, moons, asteroids and comets. Some probes carry landers, which they release onto the surface of a planet or other object.

How are probes controlled?

By computer. Some of a probe's activities are programmed in advance while others are controlled from Earth. When a probe is far away it can take hours for radio signals to reach it, so it needs to make some 'decisions' itself.

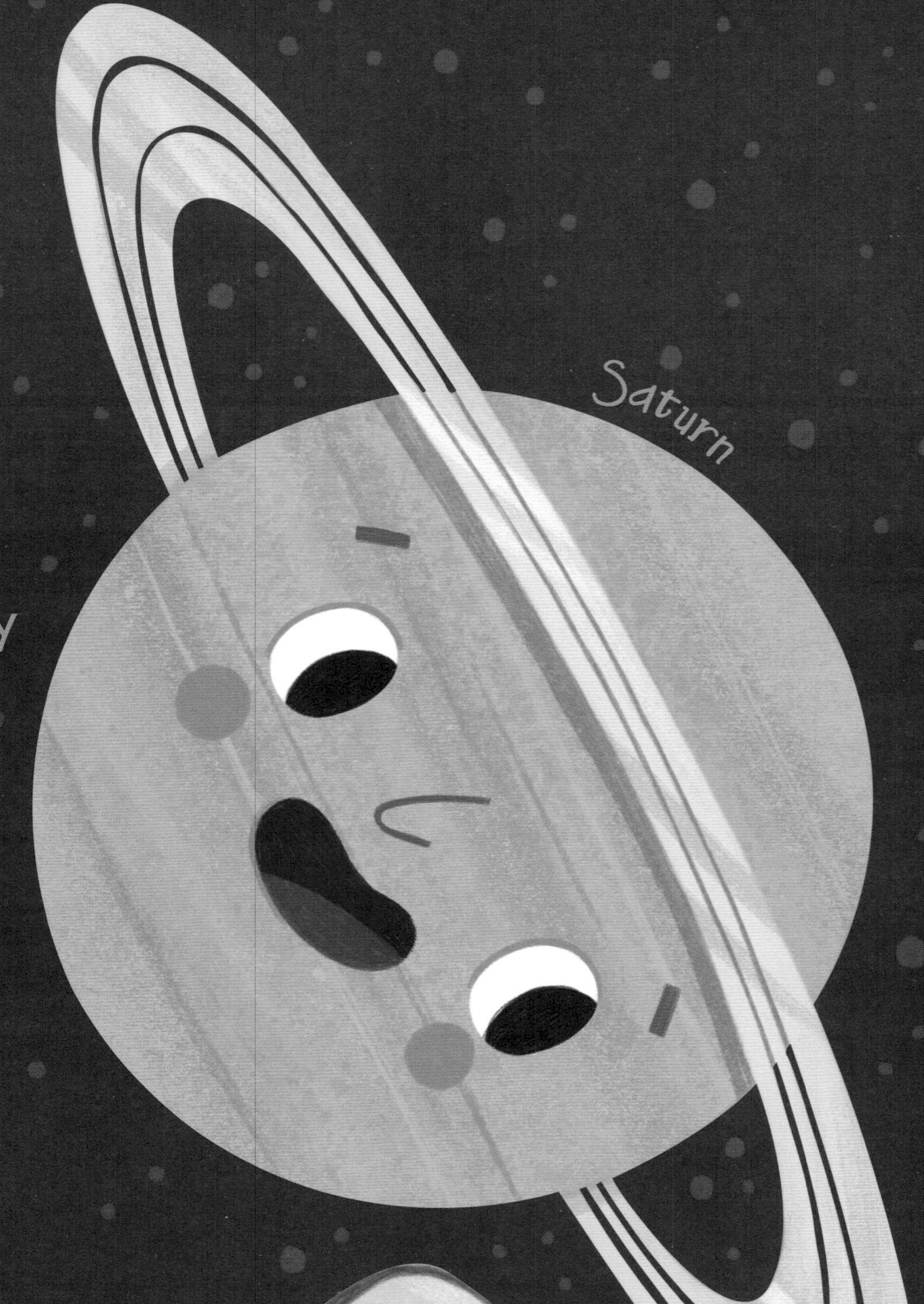

Cassini
What do probes do?
We take photos and make measurements, which we send back to Earth by radio link. I'm Cassini! At the end of my work, I plunged into the atmosphere of Saturn, making measurements on the way down!
Titan, one of Saturn's moons
What do landers do?
We take photos and collect information about conditions on the surface and send these back to Earth. I'm Huygens! I separated from Cassini and used parachutes to land on one of Saturn's moons.
Huygens

Have spacecraft been to Mars?

By 2019, 56 spacecraft had set off for Mars and 26 had been successful. Some are still in orbit around Mars, while some landers are still on the surface.

Sky crane lowering Curiosity
I use thrusters to slow me down, and lower the lander on a strong cable.

How do spacecraft get to Mars?

A rocket launches the craft into space, points it in the right direction and lets go! It takes about 7–8 months to get to Mars and the trip needs careful planning, as both Earth and Mars are moving.

How do landers land?

They use thrusters pointing downwards to slow their fall to the surface. Thrusters push them upwards while gravity pulls them down. The Curiosity rover was lowered by a sky crane!

What can orbiters do?
Orbiters look down on the whole planet as they travel around it. They measure gases, temperature and the height of the land, and take photos.
Mars Reconnaissance Orbiter
Can rovers look for life on Mars?
Yes! Rovers are landers that can move around, gathering information from different places. They look in close detail at the soil and rock, and can look for chemical signs of life.
My top speed is just 140 metres per hour!
Curiosity

Have any spacecraft left the Solar System?

Yes! Two Voyager spacecraft have left our Solar System and are journeying into interstellar space (the space between stars). Voyager 1 has travelled the furthest.

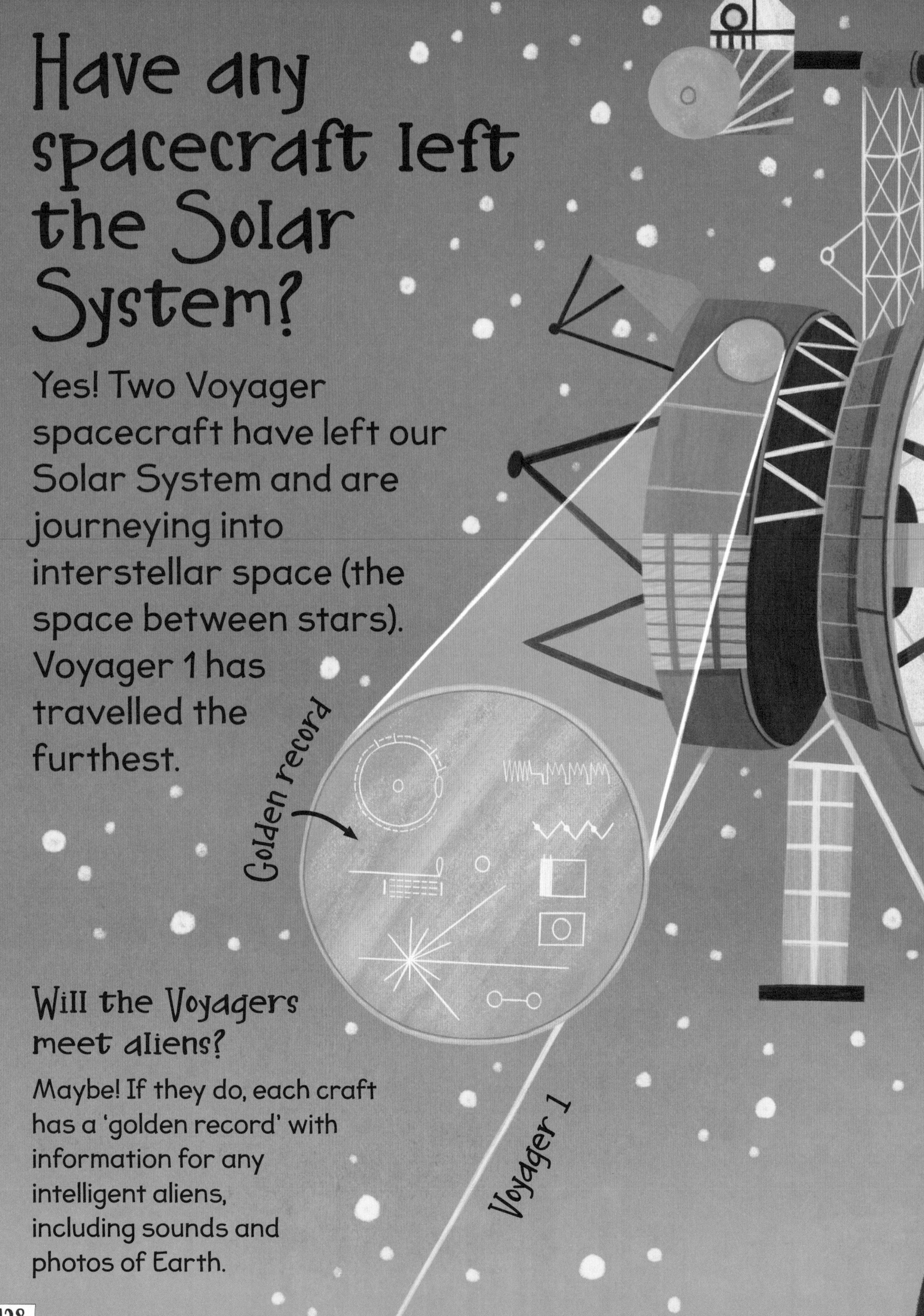

Will the Voyagers meet aliens?

Maybe! If they do, each craft has a 'golden record' with information for any intelligent aliens, including sounds and photos of Earth.

Where is Voyager 1 going?

Just to 'outer space'! In a billion years it could be about halfway across our galaxy. It will keep going until something destroys it, which could be millions, perhaps billions, of years in the future.

I'm around 20 billion kilometres from Earth! I travel at about 60,000 kilometres per hour and can cover half a billion kilometres per year.

New Horizons

Which spacecraft has visited the most distant object?

Arrokoth

NASA's New Horizons probe flew close to an asteroid in the Kuiper Belt, called Arrokoth, in 2019. It took 9.5 years to get to Pluto, and another 3.5 years to reach Arrokoth.

Did you know?

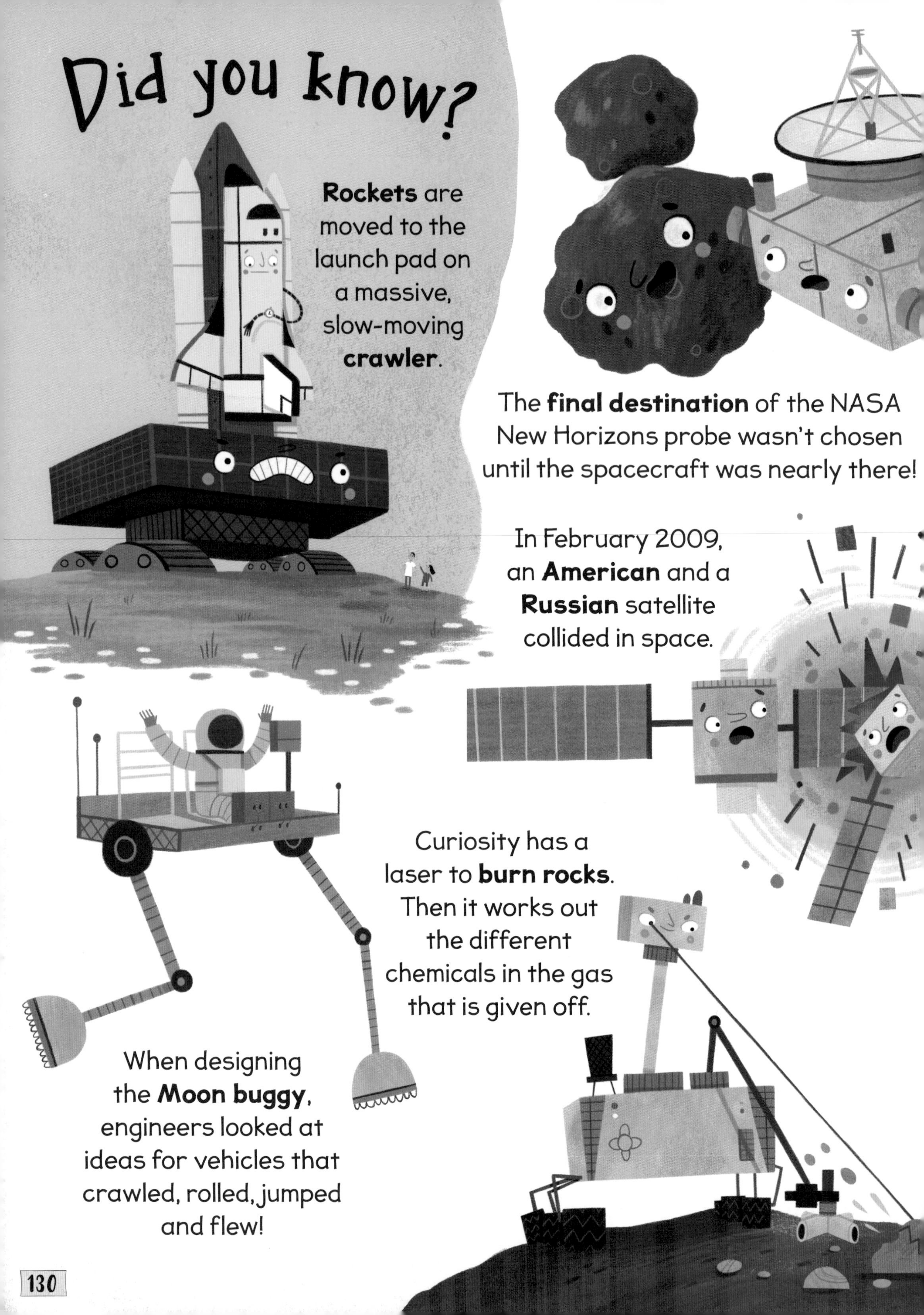

Rockets are moved to the launch pad on a massive, slow-moving **crawler**.

The **final destination** of the NASA New Horizons probe wasn't chosen until the spacecraft was nearly there!

In February 2009, an **American** and a **Russian** satellite collided in space.

Curiosity has a laser to **burn rocks**. Then it works out the different chemicals in the gas that is given off.

When designing the **Moon buggy**, engineers looked at ideas for vehicles that crawled, rolled, jumped and flew!

The Japanese spacecraft IKAROS is the first to use a **solar sail**.

The **computer** used to land on the Moon was less powerful than a modern **smartphone**.

The probe Cassini **plunged into Saturn** to avoid colliding with any moons.

There is a **Tesla car** in orbit around Earth.

The Chinese Chang'e 4 lander and rover Yutu were the **first to land** on the far side of the Moon, in 2019.

What does the future look like?

There will be lots more satellites, many of them tiny, but also more space stations and telescopes.

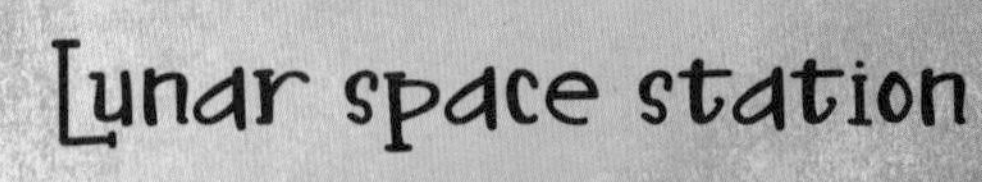

Lunar space station

There are plans for a base that will orbit near the Moon to support trips to the Moon, Mars and beyond.

Dragonfly mission

A planned mission to Titan, Saturn's largest moon, will send 'rotorcraft' to explore the surface.

I am going to investigate whether Titan can support life!

Moons of Mars

The Japanese space agency, JAXA, is planning a mission to investigate Mars' moons Phobos and Deimos.

I'm off to explore the moons of Mars.

Mission to Mercury

The BepiColombo probe, launched by JAXA and ESA in 2018, will travel to Mercury, arriving in 2025.

Sail to the stars

We could see new kinds of sails that use solar wind, radiation or even just light to push spacecraft along.

I have been built to launch heavy objects into space!

Asteroid mines

Some organizations are hoping to trap asteroids and mine them for useful metals.

Mega rockets

New types of rocket to launch heavy objects are being developed, including NASA's SLS (super-heavy launch system).

A compendium of questions

Do probes ever come back?

The probe itself doesn't, but probes can return capsules. In 2006, the Stardust probe sent back dust from the comet Wild 2.

Why have a telescope in space?

It's free from distortion produced by Earth's atmosphere and it can also pick up ultraviolet radiation blocked by Earth's atmosphere.

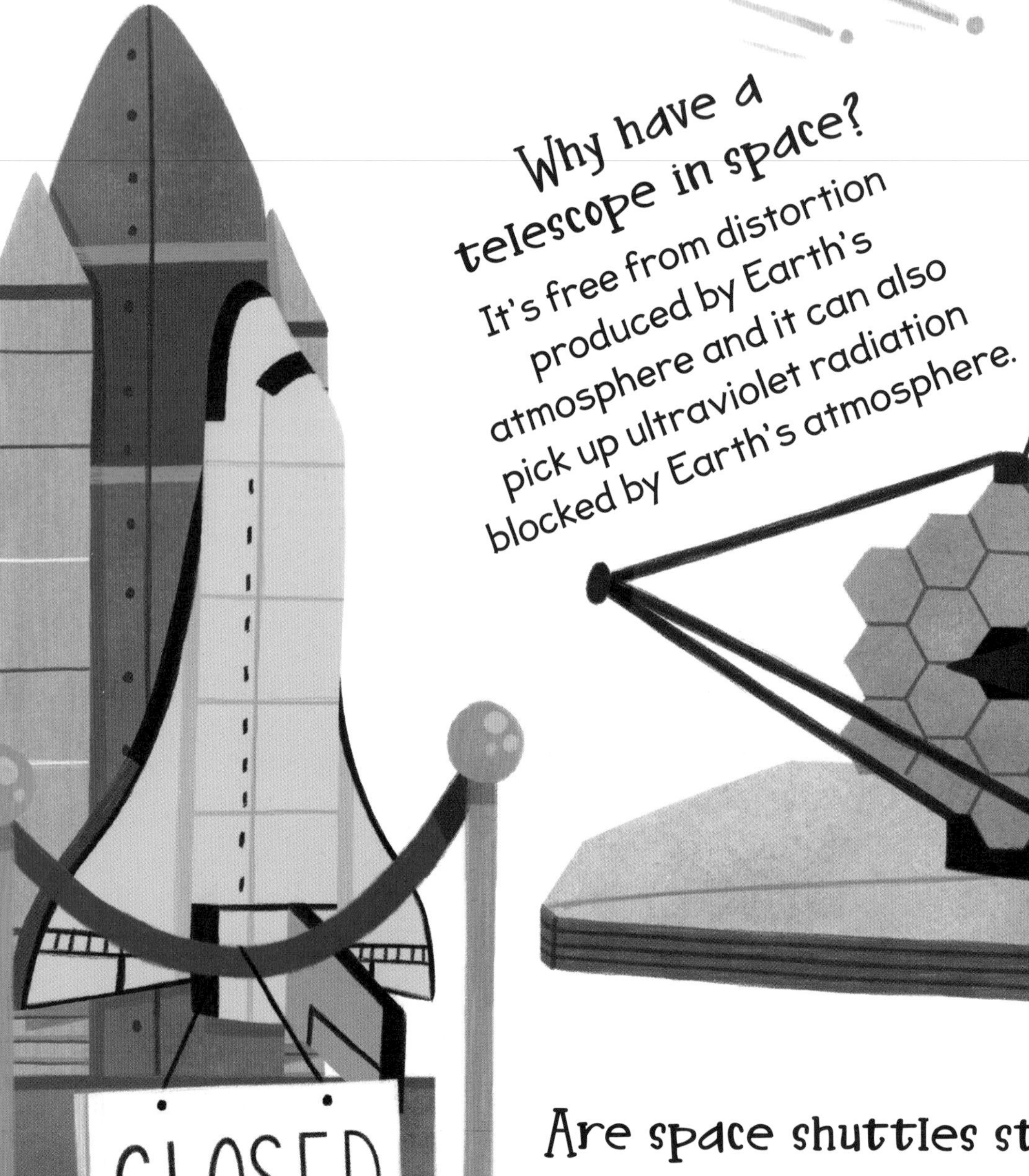

Are space shuttles still used?

No. The last space shuttle, Endeavour, made its final flight in 2011.

What does an astronaut wear under their EMU?

A giant nappy, and a body suit that has tubes to carry water and cool their body.

How do astronauts talk to each other in space?

They have a radio link, with microphones in their helmets.

Where are you going?
Out on a spacewalk!

Have we sent landers to Venus?

Yes, but they don't last long! They are quickly destroyed by the extreme heat and pressure of the planet's atmosphere at the surface.

What is the fastest spacecraft?

Juno reached 266,000 kilometres per hour in 2016. The Parker Solar Probe should manage 692,000 kilometres per hour in 2024.

How are things held down in the ISS?

Lots of things are held down with Velcro or magnets.

How do astronauts get food on the ISS?

It is sent with other supplies carried to and fro by Soyuz spacecraft.

index

Page numbers in *italics* refer to pages having only pictures of items.